Living Together

Living Together

A Practical Guide for Couples

FRANCES M WAY

KOGAN
PAGE

First published in 1995

Apart from any fair dealing for the purposes of research or private study, or criticism or review, as permitted under the Copyright, Designs and Patents Act, 1988, this publication may only be reproduced, stored or transmitted, in any form or by any means, with the prior permission in writing of the publishers, or in the case of reprographic reproduction in accordance with the terms of licences issued by the Copyright Licensing Agency. Enquiries concerning reproduction outside those terms should be sent to the publishers at the undermentioned address:

Kogan Page Limited
120 Pentonville Road
London N1 9JN

© Frances M Way 1995

British Library Cataloguing in Publication Data

A CIP record for this book is available from the British Library.

ISBN 0 7494 1433 2

Typeset by DP Photosetting, Aylesbury, Bucks
Printed and bound in Great Britain by
Clays Ltd, St Ives plc.

Contents

Chapter I

Planning Ahead

How this book can help you

People have been living together as an alternative to marriage for centuries. For many couples, living together is just as strong a commitment as being married. The law, however, has been slow to catch up with this fact. There are many inequalities between married and unmarried couples in the most important areas of domestic life – housing, personal property, children, taxation, inheritance. An unmarried father, for example, has very few automatic rights compared to a married father. A partner who does not have his or her name on the title deeds of the home may have very little rights over the property compared to a married partner in the same situation. For married couples, the spouse is the next of kin in questions of health, intestacy and insurance, whereas for a couple who are living together, each person's next of kin may be his or her parents. The list is endless.

This book shows you what practical steps you can both take to counteract these inequalities. Many methods are cheap and simple and need not necessarily involve consulting a solicitor. By taking these steps you will give your relationship more stability. A major cause of domestic strife is a sense of confusion and insecurity, particularly where money, property and children are concerned. If you discuss the issues in this book with your partner and take positive and informed action, you will be able to give each other a comparable sense of security to that given to a married couple by the law.

This book concentrates on planning your lives together, but

inevitably the issues that arise on separation are also considered. If your relationship does end, the separation will be much fairer, simpler and less antagonistic if you have planned your domestic arrangements. Living together is not a simple 'no ties' alternative to marriage. The law will give you some rights and responsibilities in some areas of life, none in others, and uncertainty in the rest. The separation of couples who lived together and have let the law decide their lives rather than make their own plans, is often far more complex and costly than a married couple getting divorced.

This book promises to avoid the use of legal mumbo-jumbo. Where legal terms and phrases are necessary, they will be fully and simply explained. Each chapter looks at different areas of shared domestic life. The book is a practical guide and does not make moral judgments or intrude upon decisions of a personal or emotional nature.

What is living together?

A couple are said to be living together when they share their lives together like a husband and wife but are not legally married to each other. Usually a test of whether a couple are living together for legal purposes is whether the couple share a home together.

The home may be rented or owned by either or both partners. The couple may have moved in together, or one of the couple may have moved in later. Either or both partners may have property in his or her own separate name as well, but they will have a main domestic home where they spend most of their time together.

In contrast, for example, a couple who happen to be sharing a house because they each have separate leases with the same landlord but who are romantically involved with each other would not be said to be living together for most legal purposes. The couple would each have separate accommodation which only that person had a right to use (although they might share a communal room such as a kitchen) and would each be personally responsible for his or her own individual finances. However, if the situation changed, for example, where they shared their private property (perhaps using one room as a bedroom, the other as a living room instead of each having separate rooms) they could well be described as living together.

In the same way, a couple who live in separate houses could begin by having a relationship with each other that gradually developed until each was sharing the other's home and life so much that they were more accurately a 'two-home' couple rather than single individuals.

Many people call an unmarried partner a common law wife or husband, and believe that a common law spouse has the same or at least very similar rights as a married person. In fact, there is no such thing as a common law spouse in English law. From time to time legislation has granted unmarried couples the same rights and responsibilities as married couples in certain areas of life. For example, an unmarried person is responsible for his or her partner's share of the council tax, just like married couples. In other areas, particularly housing, there are many gaps and uncertainties in the law affecting couples who live together. Because there are so many uncertainties in the law, it is wise to make express plans and arrangements.

There is no single legal definition of living together, and, as explained, the situation may develop gradually. For legal purposes, the definition may vary according to what issue is under consideration, such as property rights, maintenance, children, state benefits. The following is a guide to some of the characteristics of a couple who are living together. The point on living arrangements is usually crucial for most purposes, the remaining aspects need not always be present. For example, a couple need not have joint finances or a sexual relationship, just as this may be the case with some married couples.

- *You live together in the same place:* like a husband and wife, this place will be your main home and you will spend most of your time together. Either partner may have a separate home, but if a couple are usually together, for most legal purposes you will be considered as living together.
- *You run a joint household:* for example, you share household expenses and chores, eat together and share the same rooms.

9

■ *You have joint finances:* for example, you have a joint current or savings account, or you financially maintain each other or contribute towards maintenance.
■ *You have an established relationship with each other:* your relationship is serious and long term rather than casual.

Some people live together as a prelude to marriage, others as an alternative to marriage perhaps because they do not believe in it or because they are not legally able to marry due to being in the process of separation or divorce from a spouse. You should seriously consider making some of the plans suggested in this book whether you are intending to live together for a short time or indefinitely. Each situation brings different questions – how will marriage change your lives together; how will you ensure you and your partner have the same protection as a married person; how will your previous marriage and settlement arrangements be affected by living with a new partner? The following chapters will cover all these concerns.

How living together differs from marriage

Marriage is a union between a man and a woman which is recognised by the law. There are many Acts of Parliament which impose rights and responsibilities on a married couple concerning the marital home, other property and possessions, money, children, and what happens on divorce or death.

Living together is not legally recognised as an alternative institution to marriage, but there are laws which do affect a couple's relationship in some areas of domestic life, such as the care of children. In other matters, there is no specific legislation, and a couple will have to rely on the general law of the country, such as the law of property, contract or trusts.

The following is a brief comparison of marriage and living together.

Financial support

A spouse has a legal duty to support his or her partner, and the courts will enforce this if necessary.

There is no such duty for unmarried couples (however, if one or both partners apply for social security benefits, their income will be assessed jointly).

Taxation
Husbands and wives are taxed separately (since 4 June 1990) and a Married Couple's Allowance may be claimed.

Unmarried partners are taxed separately but there is no equivalent of the Married Couple's Allowance. If they have children either but not both partners may claim a special allowance for single parents.

Mortgage Interest Relief At Source (MIRAS)
A married couple may only apply for one tax relief for mortgages.

Since 1988, the MIRAS rules for an unmarried couple are the same as for married couples. If the mortgage was taken out before 1988, each of the couple will have claimed MIRAS.

Grants
A student's grant application will be assessed on the basis of both of a married couple's incomes.

An unmarried student's grant will be assessed independently of his or her partner's resources.

Property
Regardless of who owns the home, both partners have the right to stay in the marital home for the duration of the marriage. If the home is rented, both partners have the right to live in the home whether or not both are named on the tenancy agreement.

If the home is owned or rented by one unmarried partner only, that partner can ask the other to leave at any time (the court may make special arrangements if there are children).

Children
Both married parents are responsible for a child. The husband is presumed to be the father of the child and his details are entered on the birth certificate. Both parents are financially responsible for the child.

For unmarried parents, unless other arrangements have been made, only the mother has automatic parental responsibility for the child. There is no presumption that the man is the child's father, and his details may only be entered on the birth certificate under specified circumstances. Both parents are financially responsible for the child.

Wills and intestacy

If a spouse dies without having made a will, the laws of intestacy will ensure that the surviving spouse and any children are provided for.

If a partner dies without making a will, the bereaved unmarried partner is not recognised as next of kin under the laws of intestacy. If the partner needs maintenance he or she must make a special application for provision from the estate provided certain facts can be proved. A child of the deceased would be entitled to inherit automatically.

Pension schemes

Many pension schemes will pay money to the spouse and children of the policy holder.

For unmarried couples, pension schemes are usually only willing to make provision for the policy holder's children.

Separation

A married couple may live separately from each other, but a court order must be obtained to legally end the marriage. The court is able to make many arrangements concerning property, maintenance and the care of children.

An unmarried couple may end their relationship at any time with no legal intervention. The courts may make orders in relation to property and children, but they are more limited compared to the arrangements for married couples, and an unmarried ex-partner has no right to maintenance for him or herself from the other partner.

All these topics and more are dealt with in detail later on.

Quick checklist

The following is a quick checklist of the sort of matters you should try to discuss with your partner, preferably before you start living together. You will notice that most of these items are usually the main topics of arguments for both married and unmarried couples! Talking about them now while you can both be calm and objective is far better than trying to sort things out in the heat of the moment, and hopefully the discussion will avert major arguments. Next to each topic is a note of which chapters will give you information about your options. The checklist is only a guide and you may need to make other agreements to suit your personal circumstances as well.

- If you are buying property, will you have joint ownership of the home or will only one of you own the home? See Chapter 4.
- If the property is already bought, is the owning partner willing to allow the other partner to own the property as well or make a trust to give that partner property rights? See Chapter 4.
- If you are going to rent property together, will you be joint tenants or will only one of you hold the lease? If the latter, will the tenant grant the other partner a licence or sublease? See Chapter 3.
- If the property is already rented by one partner, will this arrangement continue or will the other partner be granted a licence or sublease? See Chapter 3.
- How will household expenses be paid for? See Chapter 2.
- Will you have separate or joint bank accounts or a combination of both? See Chapter 2.
- Are you going to make a major purchase of an item (eg a stereo, car, washing machine)? Will this be made jointly or separately and paid for outright or by credit arrangements? See Chapter 2.
- Have you made or are you going to make new insurance arrangements in the light of your new relationship and home circumstances? See Chapter 2.

- If one of you is or becomes unemployed, is the other able to provide financial support and take over all the financial responsibilities? See Chapter 2.
- If you have children, what are your views about their upbringing? How will they be maintained financially? Whose name will they take? Would you want to get married if you had children or would you prefer to stay as you are? See Chapter 5.
- In view of the intestacy laws for unmarried couples which do not recognise an unmarried partner as next of kin, are you going to make wills? See Chapter 6.

Many couples are, understandably, unwilling to discuss what would happen to the care of children and the division of home and property if they were to separate. However, the above topics and your arrangements or lack of them will affect both your relationship while living together and on separation should that occur, so some of the discussion is bound to envisage a possible separation.

If you wish to plan your lives together in detail, you may consider making a cohabitation contract. These contracts will also provide for what would happen in the event of a separation.

Cohabitation contracts

Cohabitation contracts are agreements by the partners which aim to regulate the financial and property aspects of the couple's relationship while they live together and in the event of separation. A couple cannot make a contract which is contrary to certain laws of the country. For example, a cohabitation contract would not be able to make rules for the provision and care of children.

A cohabitation contract should be a deed and it should be professionally drawn up by a solicitor. The solicitor will probably advise you to have both a consultation with him or her as a couple and individually to encourage full and frank discussion of all eventualities. The solicitor may decide that he can advise only one of you, and advise the other to see a different solicitor.

A cohabitation contract is very worthwhile and can be easily drawn up by a solicitor. It can deal with as many or as few matters as you wish. Common topics in a contract include:

- Property rights while living together and on separation
- Mortgage payments or rent payments
- Payment of bills
- Ownership of specific items and how items would be divided on separation
- Agreements that one or both partners will make pension or life assurance arrangements for the other's benefit

If a couple do not wish to make a full cohabitation contract, they can make a trust or special contract concerning individual matters such as the home, mortgages and mortgage deposits. Chapter 4 explains these arrangements.

Cohabitation contracts should be reviewed regularly. If there are any changes in circumstances, a solicitor could make a variation to the contract to allow for this.

Chapter 2

Your Finances

Common situations

Financial matters need to be thought about in advance, otherwise complications can arise which can cause great confusion and resentment. The following scenarios give an indication of the common situations that can occur if a couple are unclear about their financial arrangements. This chapter shows how you can avoid these situations by planning your finances. You should also refer to Chapters 3 and 4 about renting and buying a home, as rent and mortgage payments are also a major financial commitment.

When Cathy and Tony started living together they decided to keep their finances separate as they were both working and wanted to stay financially independent of each other. They agreed to pay halves for everything. However, Tony was very forgetful, and Cathy usually paid all the bills. Tony said he'd pay all the rent instead of his share of the bills, but two months later the landlord threatened them with action for non-payment of rent. Tony had mismanaged his finances and had not paid the rent, nor did he have any savings to pay the arrears.

Sally moved into John's house. As he paid the mortgage, Sally offered to buy the food. When Sally lost her job, she did the housekeeping and spent her savings on buying the weekly food and building a patio. Her savings ran out and Sally and John have decided to separate. John says as Sally lived there rent free, she is entitled to nothing.

Steve, divorced and with two children from his previous marriage, moved into Sarah's flat. Sarah bought a stereo on a credit agreement, but when she gave up her job to be a free-lance writer, she stopped making the payments and Steve agreed to pay them temporarily. Steve bought Sarah a computer and printer as a surprise, but Sarah insisted she'd pay him back when she'd written her novel. Steve's ex-wife is now pursuing him for maintenance. Steve thinks Sarah is not serious about writing her novel and wants her to sell the computer and printer and return the stereo so they can reduce their outgoings. She refuses. Steve says he can no longer afford to support Sarah financially any more and that she will have to look for a job. They want to stay together but can't stop arguing.

Why finances need to be planned

Very often a couple decide to remain financially independent of each other when they first live together. In law, there is no obligation for an unmarried person to support his or her partner. However, the longer a couple live together, the more their finances become mingled. It might happen gradually. Your partner has lost his cheque book so you agree to pay the telephone bill. He forgets to pay you back, but you don't like to appear to nag. Soon you're paying all the bills. Or it might happen suddenly: one of you is made redundant, or falls sick, or the patter of tiny feet....

Taking on more than your fair share can cause resentment and worry. While the relationship is going smoothly it may not seem a problem, but if you use up all your savings, what will happen if you want to make a special purchase or travel abroad? If your relationship ends and your partner is hostile towards you, it might not be possible to get your money back.

The problems originate from the fact that, although in principle a couple are not obliged to support each other and are considered for financial purposes as single, because of the rules of credit and banking, ownership of money and possessions may become blurred easily. Also, despite the fact that a partner cannot legally force the other partner to maintain him or her, social security rules mean that an unmarried couple's resources are considered jointly when either of them makes a claim. This could result in one partner's claim for benefit being refused, even though the claimant has no resources, because his or her partner has a good income or sufficient savings.

A major form of expenditure is the renting or purchase of a home. Chapters 3 and 4 consider this in depth. The financial support of children is also a separate topic and explained in Chapter 5. In this chapter we look at personal finances, and what you can do to ensure you both know where you stand and that one or other partner does not take on an unfair burden. Each financial topic explains what the law is, and what choices you have.

When deciding what to do, try to consider every eventuality, however remote it may seem at the moment. Consider, for example, how your needs may change if you find you are expecting a baby, or if unemployment or sickness occurs, or if you decide to end the relationship, or live apart from each other but continue the relationship. It is far better to confront and prepare for these life-changing events than worry about them and do nothing.

Bank and building society accounts

You will both probably have separate accounts at the start of the relationship. The choice is whether to keep them separate, pool your money in one joint account, or keep separate accounts but also have a joint account.

Separate accounts

If you have a separate account, only you will have a claim to the funds in it, or responsibility for the debt if it is overdrawn. If you separate, the money in that account will be considered yours. If you die, the money is distributed according to your will or to the laws of intestacy if you have not made a will (see Chapter 6) and cannot be used until the estate has been properly wound up or proven.

Joint accounts

Joint account holders each have access to the whole of the amount in the account regardless of who initially put the money into the account. You can choose whether one or both signatures are required to operate the account. Using one signature gives you both freedom and flexibility. It is handy if, for example, only one of you does the shopping or sees to the payment of bills. Using both signatures gives you more control over each other's spending.

If the couple separate, the money is divided according to the amounts each individual deposited, but he or she will need to have evidence of who put in the money.

Which to choose

If you are adamant that you want to keep your finances completely separate, you will be inclined towards keeping separate accounts. However, there will usually be some expenses that you have to share with your partner such as household bills (see pages 23–25). If you have separate accounts, you will need to rely on each other to share each bill and write separate cheques; otherwise one partner may end up paying the bills and not be reimbursed.

Joint accounts do involve pooling your money, but, if you wish, stipulating that both signatures are required to operate the account will help you both exercise control over the spending. This is a less flexible arrangement than having an account that needs only one signature, but if large sums are involved, it may be sensible to agree that both signatures are needed.

A third option is to keep separate accounts for personal use, and have a joint account for shared expenses such as bills. Each partner can decide how much to contribute to the joint account. If a standing order is set up from the personal account into the joint account, a regular sum can be deposited and the management of the account should run smoothly. The standing order is an order to your bank to withdraw a specified amount on a certain date each month (or other interval) and credit it to the joint account. You are free to cancel the order at any time and there is usually no charge to have the arrangement so long as there are sufficient funds in your personal account to make the payments.

For savings accounts, it is generally advisable to have separate accounts. Although you might qualify for a higher rate of interest if you pool your savings, separate accounts will give you absolute certainty of ownership and control which could be important to you if large amounts are involved.

Credit arrangements and debts

Many credit arrangements are on offer these days, from facilities offered by banks to individual store cards. Living with someone does not result in being responsible for that person's personal debts, but if you have a joint credit agreement or if you guarantee your partner's agreement, you will be responsible. You will usually be 'jointly and severally' liable if you have a joint agreement. This means that the creditor or person lending the money is entitled by law to sue both of you together for any outstanding payments, or just one of you for the entire amount. A guarantor undertakes to make up any deficit if the person being guaranteed fails to keep up with the payments: you should read the 'small print' of the agreement for your precise obligations.

Most credit businesses will contact a credit reference agency to see whether you are a good risk. If you or your partner have defaulted on credit payments in the past, this will deter credit companies from offering credit to either of you in the future. You can ask to see the information held by the credit reference agency and contest it if you think that it is wrong or misleading. If you are refused credit on this basis, it need not be due to either your or your partner's record. The agency checks against addresses as well as names and it could be that the defaulter was a previous occupant or someone who lives at the same address but is unrelated to you, such as another tenant. It is quite simple to correct these mistakes by contacting the credit reference agency, and you have a legal right to correct errors.

With all credit agreements you should bear in mind that the person who takes out the agreement is responsible for making the payments even if he or she no longer has the goods because, for example, they have been given away as a present.

Credit cards and store cards

Credit cards generally offer the holder a credit-free period of a month after which a minimum sum is payable or the customer chooses to pay the whole amount due. If the customer pays only the minimum sum, interest accrues on the unpaid balance, usually at a fairly high percentage rate. Store cards operate on the same principle but the card holder is only allowed to use the card for goods sold by the store. The general advice about joint and several liability and the responsibilities of guarantors given above applies. If you prefer to keep your finances separate, you will both want separate cards.

Hire purchase

Hire purchase arrangements involve paying a deposit and a fixed amount every month (or other regular interval). Until a specified amount or the whole amount is paid, the goods are considered to be 'on hire' from the company, and ownership only passes to you once the amount has been paid. This can enable the hire company to claim back the goods if the debtor fails to keep up with repayments. Hire purchase is usually an expensive way of acquiring goods due to the amount of interest charged on the outstanding sums.

Guarantors are very often needed for major purchases by hire purchase and, as mentioned on page 21, you should read all your obligations very carefully before agreeing to be a guarantor.

Personal possessions

Initially, most couples are happy to share and share alike, perhaps with the exception of some particularly prized possession. Ownership usually only becomes a problem if the couple separate. Knowing your rights may help to prevent niggling worries or resentments. If you are particularly concerned about major items, keep receipts (they are useful for repair and guarantee purposes as well).

As a rough guide, if the item belonged to you prior to living together with your partner, it remains yours. If you bought it since living together, it is yours, and if you bought it together, it belongs to both of you. The same principle applies to gifts: the item belongs to the person or persons the giver intended it for. Also, if someone gives something to his or her partner, ownership will change hands. In practice, it is often difficult to prove whether the gift was actually made, or whether the original owner just allowed the other person to use or borrow the item.

Items of value or importance should be insured. Insurance is explained on page 25.

Household expenses

There are three methods of paying expenses: one partner foots the bill, the bill is divided equally, or the bill is paid sometimes by one partner (perhaps with the other partner taking responsibility for another bill) sometimes by the other, and sometimes jointly. Usually with the third option you will find that the bill doesn't get paid at all because you both assume the other's taken care of it!

If one partner usually pays the bills, this may simply be out of necessity (see under 'Financial support of one partner by the other' on page 27). However, some partners take the view that if one pays the rent or mortgage, the other should pay the bills. This can result in very unfair property rights for the person who only pays the bills (see pages 61–62) because paying the bills and housekeeping chores are not considered equivalent to paying the rent or mortgage, even though the cost involved may be considerable.

Dividing the bills equally is usually the fairest method if both partners are working. If incomes vary considerably or if one person benefits more from the billed item than the other, you may consider dividing the bill in different proportions. A standing order or direct debit payable out of a joint account makes for hassle-free payment (see page 20). If you don't have a joint account, it may be possible for each of you to set up standing orders from your separate accounts.

Leaving it to chance as to who pays the bills and when is a recipe for arguments – no one *wants* to pay a bill! It is worth thinking carefully about your arrangements. For example, would you be happy to pay the phone bill if it emerged your dearly beloved regularly phoned his best friend in Brazil?

Gas, electricity and water bills

For gas and electricity, the person named on the bill is responsible for payment. The service company may argue that whoever enjoys the benefit of the services is also liable, but this has not been tested in court. Water rates, however, are the responsibility of whoever occupies the property whether or not they are named on the bill.

Telephone bills

The person named on the bill is the person responsible for paying it. If the phone bill causes a lot of problems, you might consider getting an itemised bill showing what numbers were dialled and how much they cost.

Council tax

A person who lives on his or her own is entitled to a 25 per cent reduction in the normal council tax. However, if you are living together you will probably be liable for the full amount (unless you are entitled to some other reduction due to a low income, etc).

Like married couples, an unmarried partner is liable not just for his or her own share of the bill, but for the entire bill. If the bill is unpaid the council can pursue either or both partners for the whole amount.

House and contents insurance

If one partner has already taken out insurance on the house and/or its contents before the other partner moves in, the home owner should check the insurance policy. Many policies require that you notify the insurance company if a new person moves into the house. Until the policy is changed, the non-homeowner's possessions will not be protected, and the homeowner's policy may be invalidated. Each partner could also make his or her own insurance arrangements.

Life assurance

Life assurance policies pay out in the event of ill health or death. Some policies provide a certain sum of money after a specified number of years have elapsed if neither of these events has occurred, with the option of renewing or altering the existing policy. The precise details depend on the particular policy.

Life assurance is a sensible idea. State benefits only provide the basic minimum. If one partner died, the other could be left with severe financial burdens, particularly if there are children to support.

A life assurance company will only make a payment to someone who has an 'interest' in the assured's life. A married partner or a child is assumed to have an interest, but there is no such assumption for an unmarried partner. While it might be possible to see the assurance profession's point of view that a casual, brief acquaintance should not automatically benefit from his or her partner's life assurance, there are as many brief marriages as cohabitations, and many couples who live together do so with great commitment and for many years.

25

Some assurance companies have a discretion to pay out to an unmarried partner, but you cannot rely on a discretion. You should check the various companies' policies before deciding which one to take out.

Pensions

Pension schemes usually make financial provisions for the pension holder's spouse and/or children if the holder dies before the spouse. An unmarried partner will not automatically receive any benefit from his or her partner's pension. If you would like your partner to benefit from your pension you should choose a scheme that allows you to nominate a beneficiary of your choice.

If a married couple divorce, the divorce settlement will usually take into account the fact that the non-pension-holding spouse will lose his or her entitlement to benefit from the pension scheme. An unmarried partner will have no such protection: the pension holder need only change that nomination and the partner's rights will be lost.

In view of the unfairness of pension schemes for unmarried couples and the fact that the non- pension holder must rely on the pension holder's initiative and good will, it is usually advisable for each partner to take out their own individual policy. Increasing numbers of married couples as well are also taking out individual plans, as they are a good investment and, should the couple divorce, an individual policy is better than relying on a divorce settlement.

Personal taxation

Both married and unmarried couples are now taxed as separate individuals, and each has his or her own personal allowance. However, married couples may apply for an additional allowance, the Married Couple's Allowance. This is initially applied to the husband's income, but the couple can choose to apply it to the wife's income.

A couple who are living together have no equivalent to the Married Couple's Allowance. However, if they have a child, one of them can apply for the Single Parent's Allowance which, together with the Single Person's Allowance, brings the individual into line with the married person's total allowance (a married person however, does not have to be a parent to claim the Married Couple's Allowance).

Financial support of one partner by the other

Even if you are both employed and financially independent now, there are many circumstances where this situation may change suddenly: redundancy or dismissal, ill health, or deciding it is best not to return to work after a child is born for example. Alternatively, you may already be aware that one partner will need total or partial support by the other.

Unlike married couples, an unmarried partner has no legal right to maintenance by the other. The low- or non-earning partner is basically dependent on the good will of his or her partner because, for social security claims, the couple are treated like married couples and the joint income of both partners is assessed before deciding whether there is a valid claim. This can be very unfair if the couple's relationship is unstable. One partner may have a high income, the other none, but because the couple are treated as one, the non-earning partner will receive no benefit and will have to depend on the other's generosity.

A married partner is entitled by law to maintenance even if the couple are not living together. On divorce, the settlement may stipulate that one spouse receives maintenance from the other, or a lump sum in lieu of maintenance payments.

If a couple who are living together decide to end the relationship, there is no 'divorce' or legal process of separation. A partner has no right to maintenance from the other, but provision may be available if the couple have children. Money and property will be divided according to the ordinary laws of property and ownership.

These are the facts and they are hard. A partner who becomes financially dependent on the other may well feel very vulnerable and worried, however strong the relationship. To save the dependent partner having to ask for money or rely on the earning partner to give him or her money, the couple may decide to change their banking arrangements.

The couple could open a special joint account to which only the earning partner contributed, but which both partners could draw from as and when necessary. Refer to the rules for joint accounts and ownership of the funds on page 20. Alternatively, the earning partner could set up a standing order from his or her personal account so that a regular sum could be paid into the other partner's account. As explained on page 19, money in that account would belong to the person named on the account. Items bought from a joint account are owned jointly unless it can be proved otherwise.

Things bought with money given by one partner to the other as housekeeping money usually belong to the person who provided the money. Again, it is different for married couples usually: as a married spouse has a right to maintenance from the other, items bought with housekeeping money are in joint ownership. Usually 'housekeeping' is only for perishable goods so this is not an important distinction, but more expensive items may be acquired if part of the housekeeping is saved.

Methods of payment for items of expenditure other than food and clothes will need to be decided upon. If the low- or non-earning partner had credit agreements or other liabilities, his or her partner has no duty to take on these responsibilities unless the agreement was made jointly. You should refer to the sections in this chapter regarding ownership (page 23) should the support-ing partner decide to take over payments: the item will usually belong to the person who took out the credit or purchase agree-ment, not the person who actually makes the payments.

If you jointly paid rent or mortgage payments together, and now one partner cannot keep up with the payments, refer to Chapters 3 and 4 for your individual responsibilities and pay-ments. It is important to keep your landlord or mortgage lender informed of your circumstances rather than let debt mount up as other payment arrangements may be possible. You may also be entitled to state benefit to help with payments.

If both partners become unemployed or if the earning partner is on a low income, you should apply for unemployment benefit, income support or family credit. Only one partner can make the application for these means-tested benefits. Unemployment benefit is not means tested and can be claimed regardless of your partner's income if you have worked for at least two complete tax years (6 April to 5 April), lost your job through no fault of your own and are now available for and actively seeking work. It is only available for one year. This period is likely to be reduced to six months in legislation currently before Parliament.

Qualification for means-tested benefits usually results in further assistance for housing costs and payment of council tax. Your local Department of Social Security office will advise you about what you may be entitled to and the Citizens' Advice Bureau will also be able to explain your entitlements.

Chapter 3

All About Renting a Home

This chapter looks first at renting a home together, and then at one partner moving into a home which is already rented by the other partner. It will explain your respective responsibilities, how the terms of the lease will affect you individually and as a couple, and how to end the lease. Public sector housing has some different rules, so this is looked at in a separate section.

Looking for a home

First you will need to make some basic decisions together such as where you would like to live and what sort of home you would like to live in. You will need to consider what sort of house or flat is necessary for your needs, and whether its location will be convenient for travelling to work and visiting family and friends. There are also several financial decisions to make:

- How much rent can you both afford? (See page 32.)
- Do you want a furnished or unfurnished home?
- Do you have the funds for:
  advance rent
  deposit
  furnishings (if appropriate)
  personal contents
  gas, electricity, phone and water supply connection charges
  solicitor's or letting agency's fees
  removal costs
  household contents insurance?

31

- How long would you like the lease to be?
- How will you share household expenses? (See Chapter 2, pages 23–25.)
- Could you manage if either of you became unemployed?

There are a surprising number of advance costs involved in renting a home. Most landlords require at least a month's rent in advance plus a deposit against damage which is usually equivalent to one month's rent. The deposit is returnable at the end of the lease, less any deductions the landlord has had to make for damage or loss to the property or its contents by the tenants.

Remember, everything in a lease is negotiable, including the rent. Have a look at comparable properties on the market to see what the going rate is for the sort of property you have in mind. Does the rent include the cost of bills, or does the tenant pay separately for these? What sort of facilities does the property offer? A house or flat that is centrally located and near transport will command a higher rent, whereas a more remote property should be cheaper. The supply or lack of a washing machine and dryer, dishwasher, and similar facilities will also affect the price, as will the quality of the furnishings and whether there is access to a garden. Do not be afraid to draw the landlord's attention to anything that you think might reduce the rent. Even if he is unable to lower the rent, he might offer to upgrade the property if it is possible.

Look for places to rent from a variety of sources so that you can properly compare prices and facilities. Houses and flats are advertised in both local and national newspapers, local newsagents' windows, universities and colleges, and by estate agents and letting agents. Let friends and families know that you are looking for a place to rent as they may be able to recommend a landlord personally or even know of somewhere that is vacant.

The lease may contain 'hidden' expenses, such as the requirement to pay for a gardener, for carpet and curtain cleaning by professional firms, and strict obligations to pay for repairs. Normally the landlord is responsible for all repairs except those caused wilfully by the tenant. However, some clauses in a lease may require the tenant to pay for specific repairs. Broken windows are a fairly common item that landlords ask the tenant to pay for. You should try to insist that windows will only be repaired at your expense if you have wilfully broken them. A tenant should also not have to pay for damage or deterioration caused to property simply by proper use over time. The lease should specifically state that 'fair wear and tear' of property is not a repair chargeable to the tenant.

It is highly advisable to consult a solicitor even though his fees will add to your up-front expenses. A lease is a legal, binding document. The terms of the lease have precise meanings and definitions which may not be readily apparent to you as legal terminology often has a different meaning to common everyday language. Your solicitor will be able to explain what the terms of the lease mean and how they will affect you practically. A solicitor will also be able to negotiate the terms for you and strike out or modify unfair or harsh obligations, and argue that terms putting obligations on the landlord should be included. Take a look at most leases and the tenant's duties will run to pages, whereas the landlord's will only be a few lines. Do shop around for a solicitor. Ask for quotes, compare prices, and if possible, seek recommendations from friends or colleagues.

If the property is completely or partly unfurnished you will need to supply the necessary furniture yourselves. Chapter 2 explains ownership of property and payment by credit or hire purchase.

If the property is furnished, you will still need to supply personal items. It is common to find that a furnished property does *not* include:

■ sheets, duvets and blankets
■ lamps and light shades
■ towels
■ mirrors
■ cutlery, cooking utensils and tableware
■ television, video recorder and radio
■ clocks
■ pictures, ornaments and plants

Less commonly a furnished property may not include cleaning

equipment such as a vacuum cleaner, brush and mop, iron and ironing board, gardening equipment and some items of furniture such as bookshelves, bedside tables, extra chairs or rugs. You should try to ask the landlord to provide these items as they can be expensive to buy and repair. If the item belongs to you, you are responsible for the repair or replacement of it should it break, whereas if the landlord has provided it, he is usually responsible for it unless you damaged it deliberately.

When you have found your new home, the landlord will want to ask both of you for references. The references are to give the landlord some assurance about your ability to pay the rent and whether you will be good tenants. The usual references are:

- bank or building society
- current or previous landlord
- employer or college reference if you are in work or education.

Some landlords may also require a 'character reference' written by someone in a position of authority (such as a doctor, lawyer, teacher, minister of religion) who knows you well. Some landlords may also enquire whether you are married. Most do not these days, but if the landlord does have any personal objections to your marital status he is not obliged to offer you a lease. It is just as important that you are as satisfied with your landlord as he is with you. You will probably have a fair degree of contact with him, so do you find it easy to communicate with him and does he seem fair minded? If the landlord is a property company, is it financially sound? Does the landlord personally appear solvent, and are his properties run well? If he has other tenants, try to speak to them.

Once you have found the property and you and the landlord are happy with each other, the details of the agreement or lease need to be negotiated, such as the type of tenancy, how long it will be, and what terms will be included.

Different sorts of tenancies

There are three main types of tenancies in the private sector:

assured tenancies, assured shorthold tenancies and tenancies which fall outside these categories. Each type will offer you different rights and obligations. The most important right affected by the sort of tenancy you have is known as security of tenure – your right to stay in the property and not to be forced to leave suddenly, and the level of rent you pay, how and whether it can be increased or lowered.

Your solicitor or local Citizens' Advice Bureau will be able to explain what sort of tenancy you are being offered and how it affects you, and whether you can request a different sort of tenancy. The following is a brief description of the different types to enable you to compare them and see what would be most suitable for you and your partner.

Assured tenancies

An assured tenancy gives you the greatest security of tenure or right not to be made to leave the property. The tenancy can be for any length of time. The landlord can only make you leave if an event occurs which is specified by the law (the Housing Act 1988) as a ground for ending the tenancy. The grounds include non-payment of rent or persistent delay in paying rent, causing a nuisance, damaging the property, the landlord needing to reconstruct or demolish the property, or the landlord requiring the property back as it was his home and he gave you a special advance notice before the tenancy began that this might occur. If the landlord wants to terminate the lease, he must follow the special procedures and time scales set out in the Housing Act.

The Housing Act also provides for the review of rents. This is done by applying to the Rent Assessment Committee for your area. For assured tenancies, there is no means of reviewing the rent for the duration of the original or first lease. But if the lease is renewed, either by the landlord simply allowing the tenant to stay on (he will have a tenancy implied by the law in these circumstances, a 'statutory implied tenancy') or by creating a new lease, the tenant can then apply to the Rent Assessment Committee to have the rent assessed.

Assured shorthold tenancies

An assured shorthold tenancy gives you security of tenure only for a certain period of time specified in the lease. That amount of time may be for the whole duration of the length of the lease, or the landlord may specify a shorter time. By law, the period must be no shorter than six months. After the protected period of time, the landlord can ask the tenant to leave simply by serving a special notice specified by the Housing Act on the expiry of the lease. The landlord does not need to show a good reason for wanting you to leave.

A tenant of an assured shorthold tenancy can go to the Rent Assessment Committee for the rent to be assessed during the original or first term of the lease, unlike assured tenancies. If, after the end of the original lease, the landlord offers a new lease for a specific amount of time, the tenant cannot ask for a further review of the rent. If the landlord simply allows the tenant to stay on after the original lease ends (an implied lease) the tenant can go to the Rent Assessment Committee. In practice, however, as an assured shorthold tenancy is relatively easy to end, if the tenant has an implied lease and he makes an application to the Rent Assessment Committee which the landlord is unhappy about, the landlord will seek to terminate the agreement.

Should you choose an assured tenancy or an assured shorthold tenancy?

You and your landlord can decide which sort of tenancy to create, so long as the property is the sort of property that comes within the Housing Act (see page 37 on tenancies which are neither assured nor assured shorthold).

To create an assured shorthold tenancy, the landlord must give you a special notice of such a tenancy which informs you briefly of your rights. The form must be completed by the landlord and given to the tenant *before* the tenancy begins.

To create an assured tenancy, no formal procedure is required, but it is sensible to record on the lease that the tenancy is intended to be an assured tenancy.

If the property is the sort of property that is covered by the Housing Act and the landlord and tenant fail to decide what sort of tenancy to create, the law decides for them – it will automatically be an assured tenancy. If an assured shorthold tenancy is made without following the correct legal procedure it will not be an assured shorthold but an assured tenancy instead.

If you are both hoping to settle into the property for a good while, say one or two years or more, you should consider requesting an assured tenancy, with the benefit of a 'break clause' (see page 44), to give you the option of ending the lease earlier if necessary. Otherwise an assured shorthold tenancy should prove satisfactory. Some landlords will insist on an assured shorthold being offered for the minimum length of time (six months) however long the tenant wants to stay, and then renewing the lease, as this offers the landlord maximum flexibility due to the lesser security of tenure of an assured shorthold, and maximum rent control.

Tenancies that are neither assured nor assured shorthold

Some tenancies fall outside the provisions of the Housing Act. The commonest reason for not being protected by the Act is that the landlord lives in the let property as it is his only or main residence. Licences are also not covered by the Housing Act (see below), but if a licence is in fact really a tenancy, the tenant will have the protection of the Act.

A landlord and tenant *cannot* agree between themselves that the Act will not apply to them: the tenancy *must* be either an assured or an assured shorthold tenancy.

Tenancies which are not covered by the Act offer very little security of tenure and no rent assessment, but the landlord must follow the proper legal procedures for evicting a tenant and must not make the tenant leave without giving him adequate notice.

Licences

Licences are not protected by the Housing Act 1988 and so the licensor can ask the licensee to leave quite easily so long as the contractual term of the licence has expired and the proper legal procedures are followed.

Some landlords try to avoid the Housing Act by calling the agreement a licence instead of a lease. The circumstances in which a licence can be granted instead of a lease are very limited, however, and if the nature of the occupation is in truth a lease, the law will judge that a lease exists instead, whatever the agreement may call itself.

A licensee has no exclusive possession of the property (which may be a house or simply a room in a house). This means the licensor has the right to enter the property at any time and the facilities are shared. A typical licence is where someone is offered lodgings – a room, some meals, and perhaps some domestic services as well.

A licence is a contractual agreement giving a right to use the property, but, unlike a lease, it creates no actual interest or right in the property which would be upheld by the law. However, the terms of the licence are binding, and if they are broken, either party may seek compensation. Many terms in a licence are similar to those in a lease, so you should consider the sections on how the terms affect you unless it says they do not apply to licences.

Like leases, a licence may be for a fixed term, or periodic. You will need to consider what sort would suit you.

The length of the lease or licence

Another decision you both need to make is how long you would like to stay in the property. A desire to settle down needs to be balanced with caution against being committed for a long time to the heavy financial responsibility of a lease or licence.

Leases or licences can be either fixed term or periodic, or a combination of both. A fixed term runs from one definite period to the next, such as from 1 May 1995 to 30 April 1997. It is advisable to insist on a break clause such as:

> ... if the tenant wishes to determine ('end') this agreement he must not give less than three calendar months' notice in writing

to the landlord and pay all rent due and observe and perform all conditions in the lease. The lease will then determine immediately after the expiration of the said notice period of three months. . . .

A licence may also have a break clause. When the term ends (or 'expires' or 'determines'), the agreement may be renewed with another fixed term, or it may continue as a periodic agreement.

A periodic lease or licence runs from one period of time to the next and is continually renewed until either party decides to end it. The period may be for any length of time, such as from month to month, weekly, half-yearly, or yearly.

The agreement

Although it is possible in some circumstances to make a verbal or 'oral' agreement, you should always insist that the lease or licence is made in writing by a professionally qualified lawyer before moving into the property. If you don't, great uncertainties may arise as to what was actually agreed and who is responsible for what.

The agreement should set out all the terms of the tenancy. You should understand the terms before signing the agreement. Remember, all the terms are negotiable. The following is a summary of common terms in a lease (and, unless otherwise stated, in a licence), what they mean, and how they might affect your responsibilities towards each other.

The parties to the agreement

The agreement will start by reciting the date and the particulars of the property, and the parties to the agreement. The owner will of course be one party, and he will usually insist that both of you are the other parties to the agreement. From the owner's point of view, it gives him protection because both occupants are accountable for the rent or licence fee and other obligations. You are also better protected if both of you are parties to the agreement.

If you do not sign the agreement, you have no right to occupy the property. At best, you may be considered to be a licensee or sub-tenant of the legal occupier who does sign the agreement (see page 45 for more information on these situations). At worst, you may be considered merely a guest or illegal occupant. This situation obviously creates in imbalance between the partners. The non-signing occupier is very much at the mercy of the legal occupier (see pages 45–46 for what would happen if the relationship should end).

The situation also makes the position of both partners insecure. This is because, although agreements usually permit the occupier to have guests now and then, they usually prohibit permanent guests. Often the agreement will prohibit the occupier from sharing the property in any way without the prior written permission of the owner. If the occupier breaks this prohibition, he or she can be made to leave the property.

It makes sense for both partners to sign the agreement. Both will enjoy the benefits of the agreement, but of course both will shoulder the responsibilities as well. Each partner will be responsible for his or her actions or omissions. It is also possible that each partner will be responsible for the other. The key words to spot in the agreement are 'joint and several liability'.

If a couple have joint and several liability, each is accountable for him or her self ('several') and also for each other ('joint'). How this works out in practice is that if one partner breaks a chair or fails to pay the rent, the owner can seek amends for everything from either that partner, or from both of them jointly, or from the other innocent partner. This could mean, in a 'worst case scenario' that you could end up being responsible for the entire rent, even though you counted on paying only half.

The benefits of being a party to the agreement by and large outweigh the risk of joint and several liability, and there are measures you can take to ensure you both remember to keep up with payments, such as paying by standing order out of a joint account. It is possible to ask for several liability only, but most owners would not agree to this as they are unprepared to take the risk of one partner disappearing and not being able to claim against the remaining partner.

Rent or licence fees and deposits

The agreement will state how much the rent or fee is and how often it is paid, and whether a deposit has been paid.

A deposit is a sum paid by the occupiers 'up front' or on the signing of the agreement. Its purpose is to give some kind of guarantee to the owner that the rent or fee will be paid and the terms honoured. The owner is entitled to take the deposit or part of it if the occupiers default on payments or cause some damage to the property. When the agreement ends, the deposit is returned, less any lawful deductions.

To be fair, both partners should contribute towards the deposit, either equally or according to individual means. The agreement should record who paid the deposit and in what shares so that the owner knows who to return the deposit to.

Rent or fees are usually paid monthly, although any period may be agreed. Sometimes the agreement specifies that payment should be made by standing order. A standing order from a bank account directly into the owner's account is generally easiest as, once it is set up, the sum is paid automatically each time it is due. If only one partner is to pay the rent or fee, the standing order will be from only one account, but if both partners pay, two standing orders can be set up from separate accounts, or one standing order from a joint account (see pages 19–21).

If the rent is paid from a separate personal account, the other partner will have no information about that account and will therefore not know if the standing order is still operating. If you have a joint account, it makes sense to pay the rent or fee from it as it is a joint expense. The rent will be paid equally if you pay into the account equally, or it will be paid according to the proportions you contribute to the joint account.

It is obviously important to have a consistent and reliable method of paying the rent or fee as arrears can be a ground for eviction. An owner will usually accept money only from the person or persons named on the agreement. Consequently, if only one of you is party to the agreement and that person fails to pay the rent or fee, the other person cannot make the owner accept payment from him or her instead. This is because it is possible the law would imply that the owner has created a tenancy or licence with the new payer. This would give the new payer housing rights (for licensees these rights will be very limited). Tenancies or licences implied by the law are often very unclear as there is no written record of the agreement. In these circumstances, an owner would usually prefer to end the agreement and ask the couple to leave if the named occupier cannot pay, or allow the couple to stay but create a new agreement which includes both partners so that rent or fees can be accepted from either or both partners.

If you have difficulty meeting the rent or fee, you could be entitled to housing benefit. You should make the application jointly as your finances will be assessed jointly.

Your landlord, if he himself is personally liable to pay the council tax on your property, cannot pass on to you his *legal liability* to pay. However, he can in certain circumstances pass on the *cost* of the council tax to you by requiring you, as a term of the lease or licence, to pay it or by increasing your rent or licence fee. Whether he can do this depends on the type of tenancy you have and the terms of your lease or licence, or what was agreed between you. Rent and licence fees are usually exclusive of water rates, gas, electricity and telephone, though some leases may specify that the rent or licence fee is inclusive of these bills. Refer to Chapter 2 for the payment of these bills and for insurance of household contents.

Obligations

The agreement usually goes into quite a lot of detail about what the occupiers must or must not do. For example, the occupier must keep the property clean and tidy, use the property and its contents properly and not wilfully damage it, and tend to the garden. Some of these obligations carry more weight than others. Wilful damage to the property may result in termination of the agreement, whereas the owner could do little in practice if the occupiers failed to do the dusting so long as nothing is damaged.

The occupiers will be liable for breach of the obligations according to whether they have joint and several liability or just several liability (see page 40). If one partner isn't a party to the agreement and causes damage, the legal occupier will be liable as the partner will be considered the guest of the occupier.

Ending the agreement

The agreement may end for several reasons:

(a) The term of the agreement has come to an end.
(b) The partners both want to end the agreement before the term ends.
(c) Only one partner wants to end the agreement whereas the other wants to stay.

The last situation involves ceasing to live together and ending the relationship or continuing the relationship but living separately. The other situations may or may not involve relationship breakdown and living separately.

(a) Expiry of the lease or licence

If you have a lease, even if the term runs out, the landlord must take proper legal action to end the lease and, until he does, you have a right to remain in the property. Consult your solicitor or local Citizens' Advice Bureau to understand your rights. If you only have a licence, the licensor should still give you adequate warning that the licence is about to expire and you must leave.

If you wish to continue living in the property, it might be possible to agree to a new lease or licence. If the landlord or licensor continues to accept rent or the fee after the expiry of the agreement, the law will consider that a new agreement has been made; in other words, the law will imply into existence a lease or licence.

Usually the terms of the new agreement will be the same as those of the old one. In the case of assured or assured shorthold tenancies, there are specific rules laid down by statute governing implied leases; with other types of tenancies or with licences, the law is not so certain. It is generally best to agree a new lease or licence in writing rather than allow one to be implied. This way, you are certain of your rights, and the agreement can be updated to reflect any changes that have taken place in your situation.

(b) Both partners wish to end the agreement early

Strictly, the agreement, whether a lease or licence, is a contract, and you, as party to that contract, are obliged to pay the rent or fee and honour the conditions of the agreement for the whole term. If you leave the property early, you are liable to continue to pay the rent or fee and see that the conditions are honoured for the entire term. If you have a fixed term, you are liable until the term expires.

If you have a periodic agreement, you must give notice that you want to leave. The notice is usually meant to be the length of the period of the agreement; for example, someone with a monthly agreement would need to give a month's notice in advance of when they wanted to leave, and someone with a three-monthly agreement would need to give three months' notice. The notice must be a complete period. For example, if you have a monthly agreement that runs from the first of the month to the next month, you must give a complete calendar month's notice – you could not give notice in the middle of the month and hope to leave four weeks later. During the period of notice, you will be liable for rent or fees and for the other obligations as usual, whether or not you actually live in the property. The agreement may specify different notice periods than the period of the agreement, or you might be able to ask the landlord or licensor to agree to some alternative arrangement.

The only way to end a fixed term early and be released from your obligations is either by operating the break clause if there is one, or by seeking the express permission of the owner and making an agreement to end the lease or licence.

A break clause is a clause in the agreement that allows the parties to end the term early (see page 38 for an example). The clause will specify what conditions must be met, for example that all rent or fees must be paid to date, that a certain amount of advance notice is given, or that all the parties must agree to the termination rather than just one party being able to terminate the term unilaterally.

If there is no break clause you must seek the permission of your landlord or licensor. He is not obliged to agree, and if he does, he may stipulate that certain conditions are met in return for his permission to end the agreement early. It is sensible to effect the termination by a special agreement so that there is a proper record that it took place and was legally valid. If the occupier wants to leave because of financial difficulties most owners will agree to end it rather than risk having a property occupied by people who aren't paying the rent or fee and couldn't pay even if sued, but check also whether you are entitled to housing benefit in these circumstances.

If there is no break clause and the owner refuses to give permission to end the term early, the only alternative is to sub-let or sub-license the property to another person. Most agreements prohibit this. If you do sub-let or sub-license the property, the new occupier will pay you the rent or fee, and you will remain directly liable to the landlord or licensor for payment of the rent or fee and honouring the obligations under your own original agreement.

(c) Only one partner wants to leave whereas the other wants to stay

The precise rights of each individual depend on whether he or she is the legal tenant or licensor (that is, he or she was a party to the agreement), the type of occupation, and whether there are any children. As with all disputes of a legal nature, it is essential that 'tailor-made' advice is sought from a solicitor or Citizens' Advice Bureau. The following is a general guide only.

The sole legal occupier wants the other partner to leave

If the partner did not sign the agreement, he or she will have very few rights (unless rights have been gained by having rent or fees accepted – see pages 41–42). It might be argued that the partner is a sub-tenant or licensee of the partner who is the legal occupier. Even so, the legal occupier could simply give the other partner reasonable notice to leave.

If children are involved, it might be possible for the partner who has no legal right to occupy to seek a court order to transfer the tenancy into his or her name if the children are to live with him or her. The reasoning behind this is that children need to be provided with a secure home and should not be unnecessarily unsettled by moving home.

The partner who has no legal right to occupy wants the legal occupier to leave

Unless the partner without occupation rights has children (in which case a legal transfer may be considered as explained above), he or she will probably be unable to make the legal occupier leave against his or her will. Always consult a solicitor to see whether you have gained any housing rights by paying rent or fees.

Otherwise, if the landlord and tenant agree, it should be possible to assign the lease to the partner who wants to stay. After the assignment the former tenant would lose any right to live in the property and would usually be released from his liabilities under the lease. Where licences are concerned, the licensor would terminate the original licence, and create a licence in favour of the partner who wanted to stay.

If the legal occupier leaves the property and no assignment of the lease or creation of a new licence has taken place, the other partner will have no right to remain in the property. He or she should try to persuade the owner to accept him or her as a new tenant or licensee. It may be possible to argue that the partner did in fact gain a right to live in the property even though he or she wasn't a party to the agreement. Legal advice should be sought in these circumstances.

The partners are joint tenants

Both partners have a right to stay in the property. If one partner agrees to move out, he or she is free to move back in again at any time. While that partner is absent, the owner could ask for the entire rent or fee from the remaining partner if the absent partner fails to pay. It is preferable that all parties agree that the agreement is transferred into the sole name of the partner wishing to stay in the property, or that the agreement is terminated and a new one made just between the owner and the remaining partner.

If one partner gives notice to surrender or give up the agreement without the other partner's concurrence, the notice will be ineffective and the agreement will continue because joint occupiers need to give joint notice.

If children are involved, it may be possible to ask the court to make special arrangements to ensure that they have a home.

Violence

If one partner has behaved violently towards the other or to the children, or threatened violence, it may be possible to seek an injunction from the court temporarily barring the violent person from the home. This measure does not depend on property rights.

Moving into a home already rented by one partner

Most leases or licences allow the tenant to have guests but prohibit the creation of a sub-tenancy or licence with another person. A sub-tenancy or licence may arise if the legal occupier permits the other person to live in the house. If the occupier breaks this prohibition, he or she may be evicted.

In some cases it is possible to argue that the owner has accepted the new partner and that a joint tenancy has been created. This may happen if, for example, the owner accepts payment of rent from the new partner.

For the sake of security and certainty, if the relationship is long term it is best to come to an agreement with the owner that a new arrangement is made and a fresh lease or licence drawn up with both partners as parties.

Local authority and housing association homes

Council accommodation is generally much more secure than private housing. Unless the rent is unpaid or the tenant mistreats the property, the arrangement may continue for as long as the tenant wishes. It is also cheaper than private housing. Some places are furnished or partly furnished, but most council accommodation is unfurnished so you will need to bear this in mind when assessing costs.

To obtain council housing, either one or both of you should apply to the local authority. Waiting lists can be long, but the authority will give you greater priority if you have a special need for council housing. It may be possible to obtain temporary housing while you are on the waiting list.

Joint or single tenancy

A couple can decide whether only one of them holds the tenancy or whether they will be joint tenants. The main impact is that joint tenants are both responsible for rent and both tenants may have a right to buy the property (both partners must agree to the purchase even if only one of the joint tenants actually buys it). If one partner is not a tenant, he or she will have no such rights or responsibilities, and little right to remain in the home if the other partner wants a separation.

If the couple are joint tenants but wish to separate, as both have a right to live in the home, the couple must come to an agreement among themselves as to who will stay. Neither partner can force the other to leave, unless violence has been used or threatened.

It is possible for one partner to assign his or her tenancy to the other. This will release the tenant from his or her responsibilities, but will also remove any right to buy the property, or inherit it on the death of the other partner.

Is renting right for you?

Renting a home involves many responsibilities. You will inevitably have to rely on each other to make a sensible arrangement for the payment of rent and the running of the house, and if one partner does not keep his or her side of the agreement, the other partner will usually be responsible as well or even instead of the partner (see page 40 on joint responsibility).

However, do not be discouraged by the complexity of renting. A good legal adviser will explain your rights and responsibilities and help to ensure that a fair agreement is drafted. Many people find that renting is a very satisfactory way of living together either as a long-term arrangement, or as a temporary arrangement before deciding whether to buy a home together. So long as you obtain an agreement with terms that are suitable for your situation, and you carefully consider the amount you can afford and how long you would like to live in the home, renting a property can provide a stable home for both of you.

Chapter 4

All About Owning a Home

For most people, buying a home is their biggest financial commitment, and bricks and mortar are usually a person's biggest asset. Added to this, a home provides security and comfort for oneself and family. It is therefore vital that all aspects of buying a home are discussed with your partner.

Sometimes this is difficult to do, but you must not dismiss the topic because you think your partner might doubt your commitment to the relationship and that you ought to just 'trust each other to be fair'. This is because, first, the law makes few provisions for unmarried couples, so you have to protect your own interests yourself. Secondly, planning how you own property will actually benefit your relationship in two ways. You will both know what your rights and responsibilities are, so insecurity is lessened and disputes avoided; and you will both be able to protect each other's future and that of any children should one or other of you fall ill or die.

This chapter considers buying a house together, one partner living in a house solely owned by the other, and mortgages and other financial expenditures and local authority and housing association accommodation.

Buying a home together

The decision whether to buy a place together or for one partner to be sole owner can seem very difficult. Besides questions of who has what money to invest, there are also issues of both partners needing security of accommodation. For some people, the decision whether to buy a home together as opposed to renting or one partner only buying the home, becomes a test of whether the relationship is serious. There are many other practical issues involved, and several options available to you, so do not let the emotional factor be the over-riding one.

Obviously, if you are contemplating house purchase you must be reasonably certain that your relationship is long term. Besides being a huge financial commitment, buying a house and selling it when the time comes is a lengthy and costly process. However, it is not just a black and white choice of pooling all your resources together and buying a home jointly, or one partner buying the home and the other partner moving in. There are ways of organising the purchase to reflect your different circumstances and needs. Equally, as explained later, if only one of you owns the home, the other partner may well gain rights to it either by taking positive steps to create ownership rights, or by trying to seek a court order granting rights.

Ownership is not simply a question of whose name is on the title deeds or land certificate (the documents which transfer the ownership from a seller to a buyer). Up to four people can have legal ownership of property, so it is possible for either one partner or both to have legal title. To be legal owners you need to be named on and be parties to the legal document. (If one of you is already sole owner, it is possible for a solicitor to transfer the legal ownership to both of you – see pages 59–61.)

If you both have legal title to the home, one partner cannot sell the property without the other's consent because ownership can only pass to a new buyer if both the legal owners are parties to the sale. In the event of dispute, the couple would have to go to court to seek an order from the judge that the property is or is not to be sold.

The legal title can be held or shared between you in two different ways. These methods can be used to reflect your financial commitment to the property if you so wish, or you may choose one method in preference to the other according to the needs of your family. The methods are called joint tenancy and tenancy in common.

It may seem strange to talk about owned property in terms of tenancies, so it is necessary to explain how this comes about. The law recognises that property can be owned outright by one person or more (the legal title); but it also recognises that others may have an interest in or right to the property because it is only fair or equitable for them to so do. This is known as the equitable title or the beneficial interest. The legal owner is said to hold the property for the benefit of the beneficial or equitable owner. The legal owner holds the property 'on trust' for the equitable owner. 'On trust' means that the person holding the title, the trustee, has certain responsibilities to use the property according to the law of trusts for the benefit of the equitable owner.

Where the couple are both legal owners, they hold the property on trust for the benefit of themselves. There are two ways or tenancies that a couple can share the benefit, and this will affect what happens when the property is sold or when someone dies: joint tenancy or tenancy in common.

Joint tenancy

Joint tenants own all of the home completely. When the property is sold, both tenants will be entitled to half the proceeds (unless the court orders otherwise in the case of a dispute where children are involved – see page 58). Joint tenancy therefore gives an equal financial stake in the property regardless of who actually paid what towards the purchase.

On the death of one partner, the property automatically passes into the sole name of the surviving partner. This transfer occurs separately from a will, so if no will was made, the surviving partner will still succeed to the property (see page 80). It is not legally possible for a joint tenant to make a will of his or her share in the property to another person: the property must pass to the surviving tenant.

Married couples usually opt for a joint tenancy, but it must be remembered that the court has far greater powers of intervention and property readjustments when a married couple separate so their reasoning could be that there is less need for them to share the ownership in any other way. You should not therefore automatically assume you should have a joint tenancy, but consider the other option.

Tenancy in common

If a couple have a tenancy in common they each separately own the property between themselves. Each person has a share of the property, and it is possible to split the ownership shares to reflect the amount of each person's investment. For example, if one person provides £70,000 and the other £30,000, or if one person pays £70 a week mortgage and the other £30 a week, one could have a two-thirds share, the other one-third. They would own the property in those proportions, and on a sale the proceeds would be divided according to those shares.

On the death of a partner, the property passes according to that individual's will, or, if he or she had not made one, according to the law of intestacy (see pages 78–81). The deceased's share does not pass automatically to the surviving partner. This gives each partner the option of naming whom they choose to inherit their share of the property. They may, of course, choose each other and achieve the same effect as if they had a joint tenancy in the event of death. Or a person could choose to leave his or her share to the children. This option may be preferred if the children are from a previous relationship and the testator wants to ensure that they benefit from the property rather than leave it up to his or her partner to cater for their needs.

If no will is made, the law of intestacy decides who will inherit. Only recognised kin inherit under the rules of intestacy. As explained in Chapter 6, a cohabiting partner is not recognised as next of kin, though children, or a spouse to whom the deceased was still legally married at the time of death, are considered next of kin. If a partner wanted to challenge this, he or she would need to contest the inheritance (see page 80). The surviving partner may be left in very difficult circumstances if the deceased partner failed to make a will, and he or she may be forced to sell the home.

It is therefore very important to make a will if you hold the property as tenants in common.

For the property to be held as tenants in common the title documents should recite that this is how the property is held, as the assumption is that it is held as joint tenants if there is no other proof to the contrary. The documents should also specify in what shares the property is held. If the property is already held as joint tenants, a solicitor can change this by serving a notice of severance on the other partner and notifying the land registry or storing the notice with the title deeds as appropriate.

Which tenancy should you choose?

If you both own the legal title, neither can sell without the other's consent. How you own the beneficial interest will determine how the proceeds are divided on sale or on death. The sale may or may not be as a result of separation, but you need to consider what would happen if you separated. How you both choose to own the property will depend on your personal circumstances and needs. Pages 60–61 look at some examples of how some couples choose to own their home to meet their particular needs, but you should always consult a solicitor for tailor-made advice.

On separation, the court can only intervene and make different arrangements from the one you have chosen if there are children. For example, if one partner is to have the children living with him or her, the court may order that the property is completely transferred to him or her in order to provide a secure home for the children. If no children are involved, the property will be divided according to whether the couple are joint or several tenants.

The factors you need to consider are your personal and domestic circumstances now and what they may become in the future. You need to weigh up each factor in relation to each other. For example:

■ How much are each of you investing in the property? Is it important to you that your relative investments are reflected in the ownership of the property? If so, a tenancy in common may be more suitable as you will be able to own the property in shares that reflect your stake in the property.

■ Do you have, or are you planning to have children together? A joint tenancy would offer greater security than a tenancy in common should one partner die. The surviving partner would become the outright owner if the property was held as joint tenants, whereas if it were a tenancy in common the partner would have to rely on the other partner making a will and bequeathing his or her share in the property to that partner.

■ Do either or both of you have children from a previous relationship? With joint tenancies, the partner's share goes automatically to the surviving partner, whereas each partner can choose to make a will in favour of the children or partner if the property is held as tenants in common.

As everyone's needs are unique, it is important that you consult a solicitor to see what would be best suited to your circumstances. It is sensible to see a solicitor together as a couple, but also separately. The solicitor will consider every eventuality, however remote, and it might be easier to talk more frankly about such theoretical situations if you are on your own.

What might happen if joint owners separated?

As joint owners (whether tenants in common or joint tenants), both of you will be entitled to live in the property and neither of you is able to sell it or raise money on it (by a second mortgage for example) without the other's consent. This means that, on separation, you would both have to agree on what is to happen to the property, or, if agreement is impossible to reach, you would need to go to court for an order directing how the property should be dealt with.

The choices open to you would be:

■ to stay living in the property together but as separate individuals rather than as a couple;
■ for one partner to remain and buy the other partner's share; or
■ for the home to be sold and the proceeds divided.

The first option is obviously fraught with many difficulties, both emotional and financial. You would need to co-operate with each other on paying household bills, the mortgage, insurance, any instalment options on furniture, and on repair and maintenance. You therefore need a very amicable separation for this to work. Matters may get very complicated if one person allows a new partner to move in. This option is usually only workable as a short-term measure, perhaps to allow time for finances to be sorted out and alternative accommodation found.

If one partner would like to stay in the property, the remaining partner will need to buy the other partner's share. In some cases it is possible to do this by adjusting the mortgage and obtaining a second mortgage to raise money to pay the leaving partner's share. The remaining partner would need to be sure that his or her income would be sufficient and that the expenses would not be too great.

How much the leaving partner's share amounts to will depend on whether the house is held as joint tenants or as tenants in common, and, if it is held as tenants in common, the proportion of each person's share. If the shares are in dispute because they were not recorded, it is possible to go to court to get a judge to determine the shares. Preferably the matter should be dealt with amicably through separate solicitors rather than going to court and incurring high legal fees.

Besides dealing with the proceeds of the house, the contents of the property will also need to be dealt with, either by sharing them out, or by one person buying out the other. The legal ownership of personal property is considered in Chapter 2.

If neither partner wishes to stay in the property, the house will be sold and the proceeds divided according to how the property was owned. Again, the personal contents of the home will need to be sorted. It might be possible to leave some items, such as the cooker, fridge and other large items, and sell them with the property.

If a couple are unable to agree what should happen to the property and whether one or other should remain there or it should be sold, a court would probably order that it should be sold and give directions as to how the proceeds should be divided. If there are children, however, the court may order that the property is transferred into the name of the partner who will be looking after the children; if there are no children, the court would have no power to order such a transfer.

One partner as sole owner

The partner who is sole legal owner of the home will have far greater security than the other partner. This is because only the sole owner is legally entitled to live in the property, and anyone else can only live there with the legal owner's consent. The sole owner can sell the property or raise money on it as he or she pleases without obtaining the consent of the other partner. On a sale, the proceeds belong to the owner (unless the other partner can prove otherwise but this is very difficult as explained on pages 61–62).

The non-owning partner has a very insecure position. A non-owning married partner, by contrast, has the right in law (as opposed to the right by virtue of the owner's permission) to live in the matrimonial home while the couple are married. A non-owning married partner has the right to register a charge at the Land Charges Registry or the District Land Registry. If a person was considering buying the home, he or she would do a search at the appropriate Registry and the charge would be revealed.

The non-owning spouse's charge would notify the buyer that the property could only be validly sold with the consent of the non-owning spouse as well as the owning spouse. The charge would also alert a second mortgagee. Before making a loan on the house, the lender would want the non-owning spouse's consent because if the loan was not repaid and the lender had to repossess the house, the lender would want full possession of it without being subject to the non-owning spouse's charge. An unmarried partner has no equivalent right to register such a charge.

The sole owner will have all the responsibilities for the house, such as paying the mortgage and any bills and repairs.

This set up may be acceptable to a couple, but usually only as a temporary situation while they wait for their relationship to become more established. It may arise if one partner already owns a home before the relationship begins, and the other partner moves in. The couple may prefer to wait to see how the relationship develops before deciding whether to sell the home and buy a new one together, or before deciding whether to alter the ownership of the property (see below). Alternatively, some couples may choose that one of them will be the sole owner.

As the relationship progresses, it is inevitable that finances will become mingled. The non-owning partner may feel that he or she is contributing towards the upkeep of the home and want that reflected in the legal ownership of the house to provide that partner with more security. For example, it would be unfair if one partner takes responsibility for the mortgage because he or she is sole owner, and the other partner pays all the bills and shopping. The owner is building up a financial asset whereas the other partner is not but may be spending just as much money on the everyday expenses as the owner is spending on the mortgage.

The situation where one partner is sole owner may arise where the sole owner is living in a former matrimonial home which has been transferred to him or her under a divorce or separation settlement. Sometimes the settlement will specify that if the ex-spouse cohabits for a certain amount of time (six months is often specified), the ex-spouse must sell the house or raise money to pay the other ex-spouse back his or her share in it. Maintenance payments may also be affected by cohabitation. The sole owner must therefore be sure that he or she can manage any likely changes in the financial circumstances if the new partner is going to move in permanently.

Adjustment of property ownership

There are two ways that the ownership of the property can be adjusted. It is possible for the owner to transfer the property into the joint names of the partners, thus giving the previously non-owning partner all the benefits of a legal owner. This can be an expensive legal process.

An alternative method is to instruct a solicitor to draw up a trust deed. The trust deed will give the non-owning partner the right to live in the home and the right to share the proceeds when the property is sold. The sole owner could still sell the home without the partner's consent, but the owner would be obliged to honour the terms of the deed of trust. If necessary, the non-owning partner could take action against the owner for breach of trust and obtain financial compensation. This possibility would probably deter the sole owner from selling the house without the other partner's concurrence in the first place. A trust deed can go into as much or as little detail as the couple wish and can be tailor made to suit the couple's particular circumstances – for example, it could include provision for children if there are any.

The following are examples of the options available to some couples in certain situations.

David and Anne are in their late forties and each have children from previous relationships who are grown up and have left home. Anne provides two-thirds of the purchase price, David one-third. As each would like the option of leaving their property to their children in their wills, they choose to buy the house jointly as tenants in common, recording the fact that two-thirds is held by Anne, one-third by David, and appropriate wills are made.

Sally and Julian have two children and are both going to pay the mortgage on their house. They decide to buy the property as joint tenants so that if either of them dies, the other will automatically own the whole of the house and be able to provide a secure home for the children.

Tania and Tony are in their twenties and have no children. Tania is able to provide a 5 per cent deposit for the house, but only Tony will pay the mortgage. Tony buys the house in his sole name, but makes a deed of trust which states that if either of them wishes to separate, the house will be sold and Tania will be entitled to the amount she contributed plus interest.

Duncan and Debbie live in a house owned solely by Duncan. After the birth of their first child, Duncan wishes to provide

Debbie with greater security, so he transfers ownership into both of their names.

Olivia is sole owner when her partner James moves in with his child from a previous relationship. James regularly gives Olivia a substantial amount of money towards the mortgage. They alter the ownership to holding it jointly as tenants in common and draw up a cohabitation contract to specify that each will pay the mortgage and that if they separate each will have the option of buying the other out, but if both want to remain in the property, James will have priority.

What might happen if a sole owner and his or her partner separated?

If the relationship ends and the owner wants the other partner to move out, there is usually very little that the non-owning partner can do. In an amicable separation, the couple may agree that the non-owner is compensated for any expenditure and that jointly owned personal effects are shared fairly, but if the separation becomes contentious, the non-owner may have few rights.

The legal status of the non-owner is basically as a guest of the owner, and the owner can ask the partner to leave at any time and enforce this by law if necessary. The non-owner may consider proving that he or she was a tenant or licensee of the owner. Even if this is possible, it will be of little help. As the owner/landlord lives in the property, the tenant or licensee will have very limited rights to remain in the property: at best he or she will simply be entitled to some notice period to give some time to make alternative arrangements and move out.

The only way a non-owning partner can establish a right to the property or its proceeds when sold is to bring a case to prove that he or she had contributed to the property in some way. Such a contribution would create a trust giving the non-owner a right to some share in the value of the house on the basis of the law of trusts. If a court found that one partner had contributed to the house, the court would deem that there was an implied intention of the couple that the non-owner would have an interest in or right in the house and that a trust could be implied by law to this effect.

The law as to whether an implied trust has been established is very complicated. Basically the non-owner must prove that he or she has made some demonstrable financial contribution to the house, such as by paying the mortgage or making expensive repairs or an improvement to the property such as an extension. Although it seems unfair because considerable expense and effort may be involved, housekeeping or paying for groceries and other such items of expenditure do not count as a financial contribution.

If the couple have children, the non-owner might be able to apply to the court if the children are to live with the non-owner. If the court decides that it is in the interests of the children to provide them with a secure home, it may order that the property is transferred into the name of the non-owner. If necessary, the non-owner could seek an injunction from the court preventing any sale of the house until the court has reached a decision on the arrangement for looking after the children and any property transfer.

Mortgages

Mortgages are the usual way of financing house purchase for most people. Lenders are usually quite happy to offer a mortgage to unmarried couples, but the rules are slightly different from those affecting married couples.

If a couple have a joint mortgage, both are responsible for repayments. If one partner leaves the property, he or she will still be responsible for the mortgage repayments. The partner who stays will be anxious to see that the mortgage payments are made in full to avoid repossession. As a joint mortgagor, the partner who stays in the house will be entitled to see a statement of account to check the other partner is still paying his or her share of what is due. If the amount is not being paid in full, the remaining partner can pay the full instalment to avoid repossession. This might not be financially possible as a mortgage is usually based on a multiple of joint incomes. If the remaining partner cannot afford to pay the full amount, he or she should explain the circumstances to the lender and pay what is possible until the situation is resolved.

If only one partner has a mortgage, that person is entirely responsible for the repayments. In practice, many non-owning partners contribute to the payments in some way, such as by giving money to the owner for the purpose of paying the mortgage, or by assuming responsibility for other bills or tasks. As explained on page 62, it is wise to have evidence of any payments towards the mortgage, and to be aware that many arrangements will not count as a contribution to the house purchase in law.

If the sole mortgagor leaves the property, the remaining partner will want to be assured that the mortgage is being paid so that he or she can continue living there. As the remaining partner is not a party to the mortgage agreement, he or she has no actual right to a statement of account which would reveal whether the absent partner is keeping up with the payments. For the same reason, the lender is not obliged to accept payment from the remaining partner. This is because mortgage payments can establish an interest in the property under the law of trusts.

In contrast, a married person who is not a party to the mortgage agreement is entitled to a statement of account and to have payments accepted by the lender because a married person has the right to live in the matrimonial home for the duration of the marriage.

Is buying right for you?

Buying a property together or moving into a home already owned by one partner has huge financial implications. The exact arrangement you decide upon together will depend on your individual needs for security of accommodation, your emotional commitment to each other, your desires to protect each other and any children you may have, and your financial capacity. All these issues must be weighed up against each other.

'Putting it all in writing' and making definite arrangements rather than leaving it to luck is, as this chapter should have demonstrated, not an indication of lack of faith, but the mark of financial responsibility and concern for each other's needs.

Because you may want to retain some financial independence, the solicitor dealing with any house purchase, transfer or deed of trust will probably wish to see you separately as well as together. This will encourage a full and frank discussion covering all the lawyer's variations of possible scenarios. The whole process should clear the air and help to avoid feelings of insecurity and uncertainty about such a vital part of your lives together: your home.

Home ownership has many advantages over renting. You are building up an asset rather than just spending money on rent. You can live in the home for as long as you like rather than for as long as the lease allows, and you can live in it exactly the way you choose rather than being subject to a landlord. However, because of the financial commitment involved, you need to be sure that your relationship is stable enough to make ownership worth while.

Some rents may be as high as monthly mortgage payments, but if you rent you will not be responsible for repairs and main-tenance, and if the property is furnished you will not have to buy furniture. Renting is also a more flexible option if you are not sure you want to stay in an area for very long. You can try out the area by having a short lease, and if you are not satisfied with it (or the house or neighbourhood) it is comparatively simple and cheap to move at the end of the lease as compared to selling a house or flat. Do not automatically rush into home ownership, but consider the option of renting and the issues raised in Chapter 3 on renting property.

Chapter 5

Children

Nearly as many children are born to unmarried parents as married parents these days. The stigma of 'illegitimacy' is practically non-existent. However, the law affecting unmarried parents is different from that affecting married parents – the principal difference is that an unmarried father has to establish his rights as a parent, whereas a married father has automatic rights.

This chapter will look at the rights of parents and children and what you can do to ensure that your rights are protected. The Children Act 1989 aims to treat parents equally regardless of sex or marital status. The new rules introduced by this Act and how they will affect you and how you bring up your child will be explained. Financial aspects of raising children are considered, including the Child Support Act 1991.

The birth and registration

All hospitals are happy for any person close to the mother-to-be to be present at the birth. The only exception is if it is necessary for an emergency caesarean to be performed and the mother has to have a general anaesthetic. A partner or friend or a member of her family may usually be present at a caesarean performed when the mother only has an epidural anaesthetic during which she remains fully conscious.

Not later than six weeks after the birth, the child's details must be registered at the registry office which is local to the place of birth. If it is not possible to register the birth at the local registry, the birth can be registered quite simply at any registry office by making a special declaration on a form provided by the registry.

Who can register the birth?

For married couples, either parent may register the birth. A married man is automatically assumed to be the father of his wife's child and he has the right to have his details entered on the birth certificate. An unmarried father is not presumed to be the father of his partner's child and has no such right to have his details on the birth certificate. An unmarried father's details may be given if both the parents agree to it and sign the register. Alternatively, the father alone can give the details and sign the register if he presents a sworn statement by himself acknowledging paternity, and a sworn statement by the mother acknowledging that he is the father. A solicitor will swear a statement for a small fee.

Without the agreement of the mother, the only way a father can have his details noted is by presenting a court order to the registry that shows he has parental responsibility for the child (see pages 67–69 for the meaning of parental responsibility).

The birth details are:

■ the baby's name, sex and date and place of birth;
■ the mother's name, and, if applicable, any former name such as a maiden name;
■ the mother's birth details;
■ the mother's occupation may also be entered on the certificate;
■ if applicable, the father's name, birth details, address and occupation.

All relevant information must be given to the registry, but there are two forms of certificate showing different amounts of detail. The short form certificate is free and states only the baby's details. The longer form, for which you have to pay a few pounds, shows parental details as well.

The baby's name

Although the birth must be registered within six weeks, the name of the baby can be entered or altered by the registry on the certificate within a year of the birth. Additional names, such as a baptismal name, can also be entered within the year. After a year, a name can be changed only if there is some written evidence that it was the baby's true name during his or her first year of life.

There is no legal requirement that a baby takes his or her father's surname, and this is so even if the parents are married. A surname is not proof of paternity on its own. However, having the father's surname may be used as evidence of paternity in maintenance proceedings and may assist the father in obtaining various orders from the court such as a parental responsibility order (see pages 67–69) or orders relating to which parent the child lives with and regulating contact with the father.

How will the parents' marital status affect the baby?

Children are now referred to as being the offspring of unmarried parents rather than as illegitimate. This is because the Family Law Reform Act 1987 removed nearly all the legal discrimination against so-called illegitimate children. The parents' unmarried status affects their rights and responsibilities, principally the father's rights, rather than the rights of the child. However, marital status does influence a child's nationality. A child of married parents takes his nationality from both parents. A child of unmarried parents takes his nationality from his mother only.

If the parents marry after the child is born, the father will obtain all the rights a married father has. The next section looks at these rights and the duties of parents.

Parental responsibility

Parental responsibility is a term introduced by the Children Act 1989 and is used to refer to the usual rights and responsibilities a parent has towards a child, such as making decisions about the child's education or medical treatment.

The law grants both married parents responsibility for their child, whereas for unmarried parents, only the mother has legal responsibility. In practice, if the parents are living together, both of them will be involved in bringing up the child and making decisions about his or her future. However, the father has no actual automatic rights, and instead must take positive steps in order to obtain them.

If the father does not take any steps towards obtaining parental responsibility, the mother will be free to make all decisions about the child, such as where he or she goes to school, where and when they go on holiday, whether the child moves home. The father can obtain rights, and when the child is sufficiently old enough to understand, the child can enforce rights as well.

A father can obtain parental responsibility by:

■ making a parental responsibility agreement with the mother; or, if there is no agreement
■ asking the court for a parental responsibility order.

Parental responsibility agreements or orders do not take away the mother's automatic responsibility. An agreement or order may be revoked by the court, but only if there are very strong reasons to suggest the arrangement is not in the best interests of the child.

Parents who both have responsibility for the child need to make joint decisions about matters affecting the child. If the decision is important and the parents cannot agree with each other, they can go to court for an order. The court can make a 'prohibited steps' order to prevent something happening, or a 'specific issue' order ordering something to take place.

Common prohibited steps orders are to prevent a parent taking the child outside the UK without the other parent's consent (or without the court's consent). An example of a specific issue order could be for certain medical treatment to be given to the child as it is, in the opinion of the court, in the child's best interests whereas one parent may have tried to prevent it on religious or ethical grounds. The court's decision is always based on what would be in the best interests of the child according to his or her needs, rather than the parents' needs or wishes.

A parental responsibility agreement must be made in a form

prescribed by law. Blank copies of the form are available from local divorce county courts. It is sensible to obtain legal advice prior to making the agreement, as it has important legal implications for both parents. A parental responsibility order can be obtained by making an application to the court on a court form. The form shows the name of the mother and her address, and the father's name and address. A declaration is made that both parents agree that the father will have parental responsibility in addition to the mother's responsibility. The child's name, sex, date of birth and date of the eighteenth birthday are recorded. The significance of the eighteenth birthday is that the agreement will cease when the child reaches the age of 18. The only other way a parental responsibility agreement can be terminated is through the court, either on application by a parent with responsibility, or by a child with the court's leave (or permission). The form has to be signed and dated by both parents and witnessed, and filed at the Principal Registry of the Family Division, whose address is printed on the form.

Instead of or in addition to obtaining a court-registered parental responsibility agreement or order, the parents can make a simple written agreement between themselves. This informal agreement can go into as much or as little detail as the parents wish about the child's upbringing. This agreement would not have any legal force and does not give the father any legal rights. It can, however, be used to provide evidence to the court of what is the child's and the parents' usual practice should any matter be in dispute before the court (in such a case, the court would not disrupt the child's routine without good cause).

Residence

If the parents are unmarried and only the mother has parental responsibility because the father has not obtained a parental responsibility agreement or order, the child will live with the mother. If the parents separate and the father wants the child to live with him, he would need to apply for a residence order from the court.

The court would decide what is in the child's best interests and would consider what the child is used to, and, if the child is old enough, what the child prefers. A child who is considered by the court as capable of understanding the issues involved may make an independent application to the court about his or her preferred residence. Usually, for the sake of convenience, the child lives with one parent only and has regular contact with the other parent, but the court does have the power to specify that the child lives with both parents alternately and to state how long the length of stay with each parent would be. For example, one parent might look after the child during the week, and the other parent at the weekend.

If the father successfully sought a residence order, he would also obtain a parental responsibility order if he had not already done so. This would not affect the mother's parental responsibility.

Questions of who the child lives with may not seem relevant while the couple are happily living together, but it is worth being aware that, unless a father has a parental responsibility agreement, it is automatically assumed in the first instance that the child will live with the mother. For some couples, this inequality may be important enough to them to be a reason for getting married once they plan to have children.

Contact

Contact with a parent is another issue where the mother is automatically favoured in the first instance. If the parents separate, a mother who has sole parental responsibility is able to decide who the child sees, where the child sees that person, and for how long the visit lasts. This includes whether the child sees the father.

If the separation is fraught, the mother may refuse to let the child visit the father. Both the father and the child (if he or she is old enough to understand) may ask the court to make a contact order. The order gives the child the right in law to see the parent named on the order and to have other usual forms of contact such as telephone calls and letters. Either parent can be specified in the order, so if the father has obtained a residence order, the contact order can be for the mother to visit. A contact order may simply state the right to contact, but if the courts consider it necessary, it may also specify how much contact is to be allowed and when it takes place.

Financial maintenance

Although unmarried partners have no legal responsibility to maintain each other, both are responsible for maintaining any children. If one partner fails to provide maintenance, the other partner can apply to the court to force the partner to pay.

The new government body responsible for assessing and ordering maintenance is the Child Support Agency (CSA) which was set up by the Child Support Act 1991. The CSA's role is to ensure that a parent who is not living with the child makes a contribution to the upkeep of his or her child. The parent with whom the child lives is known as the parent with care and is entitled to make an application to the CSA. If the parent with care is receiving state benefit, such as income support or family credit, the CSA will approach the parent with an enquiry as to the identity of the child's father and his whereabouts. The parent with care is only allowed to withhold this information in very limited circumstances, such as a strong possibility that the information would lead to violence or severe distress for the parent with care or the child.

The CSA calculates how much maintenance an absent parent should pay by using a prescribed formula. The parent with care is not entitled to maintenance for him or herself. The Department of Social Security (DSS) will provide a booklet setting out the basic formula so you can make a rough estimate, or you could ask your Citizens' Advice Bureau to advise you what sort of amounts are likely to be involved.

The formula is meant to take into account the financial commitments the absent parent already has, but there has been much criticism about the formula and whether it does allow for all necessary outgoings such as pensions or life assurance, and that the level of maintenance ordered leaves the absent parent on a very low income.

If either parent disagrees with the decision, he or she can ask for a review and, if that review is unsatisfactory, ask for an appeal to the Child Support Appeal Tribunal. A further appeal can then be made to the Child Support Commissioners but only in very limited circumstances such as where the tribunal has made a mistake as to what the law means.

If either parent's circumstances change, he or she may apply to the CSA for a review of the maintenance in the light of the changed circumstances; otherwise a review is carried out by the CSA each year to check that their information is still up to date.

If an absent parent fails to pay maintenance, there are various methods that the CSA can use to force an absent parent to pay, such as an order to deduct the maintenance from the absent parent's income. Ultimately the court can issue a warrant for payment and order imprisonment for up to six weeks.

The government has recently announced changes to the way maintenance is calculated by the CSA. It remains to be seen whether these changes are sufficient to satisfy the many critics. It is likely that more changes will follow. The CSA has proved unpopular in its operation, but the principle of a parent paying for his or her children is accepted by most.

Adoption

Two unmarried people cannot jointly adopt a child like a married couple. Instead, one partner would have to make an application for adoption on his or her own.

If an unmarried mother wanted to give her child up for adoption and the father had not taken action to acquire parental responsibility (see pages 67–69), the adoption could proceed without the father's consent. Adoption severs the natural parent's parental responsibility, so a court would make enquiries to ascertain whether the father wanted to claim parental responsibility before ordering an adoption without his consent.

A father who objected to the adoption could establish parental responsibility and seek a residence order so that his child would be able to live with him instead of being adopted.

If a parent caring for a child has a new relationship or gets married to someone other than the child's parent, the new partner is unlikely to be allowed to adopt the child as his own. This is especially so if the child has established a relationship with the non-resident parent.

Issues that arise when a couple have children

Having children obviously involves a couple very closely emotionally, both with each other and with their child. The status quo of the relationship is always changed by the arrival of children. For example, one partner may give up work to look after the child and become financially dependent on the other partner. The child will need a secure home as frequent moves would disrupt his or her education and social development. For these reasons, there are many laws relating to the care and maintenance of children.

The arrival of children will inevitably bring about changes in your needs and priorities. It is a time when couples may consider getting married. Fathers especially may be aware that the law gives an unmarried father few rights and they may object to this inequality. Marriage would automatically give the father parental responsibility, and it would also provide the mother with greater property rights and entitlement to maintenance for herself as well as for her child if the couple later separated.

Couples who decide to remain unmarried when they have children should consider whether they should make a parental responsibility agreement and an informal agreement about the child's upbringing in order to give the father more rights. It may seem overly cautious to make such arrangements, and a partner may question the other partner's commitment to the relationship if asked to make a legal agreement; but without such action, the unmarried father is in a very different position from a married father. An awareness of this inequality may itself cause friction within a relationship, whereas making your own provisions for parental responsibility and issues of upbringing may get everything out in the open and be a good opportunity for discussing your views on how to bring up your child.

Couples should also consider reviewing their financial arrangements and property ownership once they have children, to reflect their changed circumstances and needs. Now would be a good time to consider making a cohabitation contract (see pages 14–15) if they have not already done so. They should also make wills to protect each other and provide for their children. Children of intestate parents (intestate means someone who has not made a will) can inherit from their parents, but an unmarried partner is not automatically entitled to inherit. The next chapter considers wills, and also the appointment of guardians to look after children.

Chapter 6

Matters of Life and Death

No one likes to dwell too much on the sadder side of life; there is sometimes even the thought that if you don't think about it, it won't happen. Nevertheless, each and every one of us is subject to life's uncertainties. Some plans and provisions in the event of death or illness show care and consideration for one's nearest and dearest so that if the worst does happen, at least some of the practical and financial problems are eased.

A lot of people assume that state benefits will be adequate in the event of illness, and intestacy laws will ensure that loved ones inherit. This is far from true. State benefits only provide for very basic living standards. As regards intestacy, unmarried couples especially need to make plans.

Professional advisers

If you want to make a will you should consult a solicitor. Homemade wills are often completely or partially invalid. A solicitor will also help you to organise your affairs to minimise inheritance tax. A will can also be used to appoint a guardian to look after children, and to set up a trust to provide maintenance for children.

Financial services is a booming area of business and you have probably been sent information about personal pensions and life insurance through the post and may even have been approached by a local personal financial adviser. High Street banks and building societies all offer advice and products. Very often the adviser has an incentive to promote one scheme above another because of bonuses or commission paid to him. You need to be sure that the advice offered is independent, properly tailored to your needs, and given by someone who is properly qualified, experienced and authorised.

Any adviser you are considering should be authorised by either LAUTRO, FIMBRA or the PIA. The PIA (the Personal Investment Authority) will take over responsibility for authorising financial advisers from LAUTRO and FIMBRA in October 1995, and until then you should check that the financial adviser is authorised by at least one of these bodies. You can check the authorisation of a financial adviser by enquiring of the Securities and Investments Board's central register. Their address is Gavrelle House, 2–14 Bunhill Row, London EC1Y 8RA (0171-638 1240).

The rule when using professional advisers is to check they are authorised and to shop around. This will help you to compare prices as well as let you see what range of services and products is available.

Health issues

As explained in Chapter 2 (see pages 25–26) it is possible to take out insurance against ill health, injury or death, but unmarried couples need to check that their partner can be nominated as beneficiary as this is not always automatic. Such policies are well worth considering because state benefits are minimal whereas an insurance policy can go a long way towards maintaining one's usual standard of living.

Innumerable types of policies are available and it is important to consider what would particularly suit you. Some policies are 'free standing', others may be attached to a mortgage agreement. You can choose how much you would need in the event of illness or death, and the level of your monthly payments needed to provide this protection. Plans can usually be reviewed at intervals to allow for changing personal and financial circumstances.

Medical consent

Medical procedures require the consent of the adult undergoing treatment. For treatment of children, the consent of a parent is needed except in an emergency.

If an adult is incapable of giving consent because, for example, the person is unconscious, a doctor is able to treat the patient if delay would result in serious deterioration or death. Otherwise, an application would need to be made to the court as to whether medical intervention is in the best interests of the patient.

Next of kin and confidentiality

In matters of sterilisation or abortion it is common practice for the medical practitioner to have a consultation with the patient's wife or husband, while respecting the patient's right to confidentiality, as the spouse would obviously be affected by such a decision to have treatment. However, a hospital is less likely to enquire about whether an unmarried partner of a patient should be consulted. This could simply be because the hospital may not realise that the patient has a partner. The patient is, of course, free to ask his or her partner to be present at the consultation if desired.

All hospitals enquire who the patient's next of kin are in case they need to be contacted. For married couples, the spouse is the next of kin, but for unmarried couples it is usually the patient's parents. Some hospitals will try to refuse a patient just naming an unmarried partner and ask for parents to be named as well. But most hospitals will accept an unmarried partner as the next of kin in practice as so many couples live together rather than marry, and it may be impractical to contact parents who might live a long way away whereas the partner actually lives with the patient.

Medical treatment for children

For children, the consent of a parent is needed for any medical intervention (except in emergencies). This includes preventative treatment such as vaccination as well as treatment for an existing complaint. If the father has not acquired parental responsibility the mother, who automatically has parental responsibility (see pages 67–69), can make the decision alone whether to approve treatment or not. For parents who both have responsibility but disagree about whether the child should have treatment, the court can be asked to make an order as to what the decision should be on the basis of the child's best interests.

Wills and intestacy

A common misconception is that when someone dies intestate (without having made a will) the rules of inheritance are sufficient, especially if you don't have a great deal of money or assets. In fact, there are many reasons why making a will is sensible:

- You can decide who inherits what and make special provision for people who would not be included in an intestate distribution.
- You can make specific bequests of particularly important items to people; for example, you can choose who inherits the 'family heirloom'.
- You may be able to lessen inheritance tax by careful planning.
- You can set up trusts to provide for children during their childhood.
- You can appoint guardians to care for your children after your death.
- You can make 'mutual' wills or complementary wills with your partner (see pages 82–84) so that the terms do not illogically conflict with each other.

These points are valid whether or not you are married, but unmarried couples in particular should make wills because the laws of intestacy are very unfair and can result in severe financial hardship and distress.

Intestacy

If someone dies intestate the law specifies how the estate is to be distributed. This covers a person who has not made a will as well as someone who has made a will but it is declared partly or completely invalid due to some legal inaccuracy. There are many rules about how to make a valid will, so it is essential to consult a solicitor rather than attempt to make one by yourself.

Under the laws of intestacy, the estate is distributed proportionately among the intestate's next of kin. An unmarried partner is not recognised as next of kin and receives no benefit from the estate. The order of the next of kin is, in summary, as follows:

- a legally married spouse (as opposed to an ex-spouse)
- children
- parents
- brothers and sisters and half-brothers and half-sisters
- grandparents
- uncles and aunts
- the Crown.

A legally married spouse means someone the intestate was married to at the time of death and not a spouse from whom he or she was divorced or legally separated. If the intestate had only informally separated from his or her spouse but was still actually married, the spouse would inherit, even if the intestate had been living with a new partner.

A spouse inherits the estate up to a certain amount (which is set periodically by the government). If there is anything remaining, the children would inherit; but if there are no children, there are no limits on how much a spouse may inherit and the spouse will inherit the entire estate.

If the intestate has no spouse, the children inherit equally. If there are no children, the other relatives inherit according to the order of the next of kin.

A child is entitled to inherit from his parent regardless of whether his parents were married or not. The estate would be held in trust until the child reaches the age of 18. This means that while the child is a minor, someone will be appointed as a trustee to look after the assets on behalf of the child until he is an adult.

For unmarried couples who don't make a will, this could mean that the parent left looking after the child may find it difficult to have access to the money for the child's benefit, and is unable to make use of the trust for his or her own maintenance. Maintenance of the surviving parent may, of course, be essential in order that the child is properly looked after. The parent would, for example, need to have somewhere to live and would need sufficient income for living expenses.

The only way an unmarried partner would be able to receive some of the estate would be to make a special application to the court for consideration under the Inheritance (Provision for Family and Dependants) Act 1975. There is no guarantee that an application will be successful and the partner would need to prove that he or she was financially dependent on the intestate. Making a will and providing for your partner would avoid all this distress.

Making will

It is essential to make a will if you would like your partner to inherit, as the laws of intestacy will not provide for him or her (see pages 78–80).

It is important to consult a solicitor when you make a will because there are many legal technicalities which must be observed, otherwise the will may be declared invalid. Your solicitor will ensure that you have considered every aspect of making a will and can help you to plan your affairs to minimise inheritance tax. Inheritance tax is payable on an estate after the first £150,000 (the level is revised from time to time in the Budget). Bequests to a spouse are not subject to any inheritance tax whatever the value, but a bequest to an unmarried partner has no such exemption.

Not all assets can be disposed of by will. Property held as joint tenants will pass to the surviving person who held it jointly with the deceased. As explained in Chapter 4, the property passes automatically to the surviving joint tenant. If the home is held as tenants in common, each person can distribute his or her share as he or she chooses (or according to the laws of intestacy if no will is made). If a couple own their home as tenants in common and the deceased did not make a will, the surviving partner may well find that he or she has to share ownership of the house with the deceased's relatives. This usually means the property must be sold, and it can impose severe financial difficulties on the surviving partner who may not be able to afford to buy the relatives out. It is therefore very important to make a will and provide for one's partner.

To provide for a child under 18 years old, the testator could set up a trust in the will for the benefit of the child. The trust can specify how the money is to be used and for what purposes. The testator can choose anyone to be the trustee of the trust, but should obviously consult them and obtain their consent first.

Setting up a trust can prove to be a reliable way of providing for children who do not have the testator's partner as their other parent if the testator is concerned about leaving it to his or her partner's discretion as to how to provide for the testator's children. The testator may, for example, be concerned that the surviving partner's priorities could change if he or she forms a subsequent relationship and possibly have children from that relationship.

A will can also be used to appoint guardians to look after the child in place of the parent.

Who looks after the children?

As explained on pages 67–69, only a mother automatically has parental responsibility and care of the child. This means that, if she dies and the father has not obtained parental responsibility, he would need to apply to the court for a parental responsibility order to look after the children after her death. A father who already has a parental responsibility order or agreement at the time of the mother's death will automatically be able to look after the child.

A guardian is someone nominated by the parent to look after the children after the parent's death. The guardian takes the place of the parent and cares for the child and makes decisions about his or her upbringing as a parent would. It is therefore important to choose a guardian whom you consider trustworthy and who holds similar views on parenting to yours.

No one has to be a guardian just because they have been nominated to be one in a will. Obviously, you would need to discuss the matter very carefully with a prospective guardian before making your will, and satisfy yourself that he or she would take their responsibilities seriously.

Any parent who has parental responsibility can appoint a guardian. The parents could, of course, appoint each other as guardians. While it may help a father who has no parental responsibility and therefore no automatic right to look after the child, it would be better for the father to obtain parental responsibility and for both the mother and father to appoint separate guardians. This is because a guardian only steps in if there is no surviving parent with responsibility able to care for the child. Appointing a separate person as guardian will not, therefore, take away the surviving parent's right to care for his or her child, but will provide for the possibility of both parents dying at the same time.

What happens when the father has not obtained parental responsibility and the mother has appointed someone else as guardian? If the father is able to obtain a parental responsibility order and residence order from the court, he will take precedence over the guardian. If the deceased parent has not appointed a guardian, the surviving parent is entitled to look after his or her child, but would need to apply to the court for a parental responsibility order if the surviving parent did not have parental responsibility at the time of the parent's death.

If the surviving parent is unable or unwilling to care for the child, it is possible for another relative or someone close to the child to apply to court to look after him or her. The local authority would take the child into care if there were no willing relative in this situation.

Making wills together

It usually makes sense to discuss your wills with each other as there will be many areas which will need joint decisions, such as the appointment of guardians for children. Each person will make an individual will, but it is possible to make wills that are complementary with each other, or that are 'mutual' in that they contain similar terms. This could avoid the following situations, for example:

Molly makes a will leaving everything to her partner Bob, but Bob doesn't make a will. Molly dies first and Bob inherits, but a few years later Bob has a fatal accident. The next of kin are Bob's parents, so they inherit everything. Molly may have preferred that her own aged parents received something too.

Simon decides that he would like Sally to have their country home after his death, but that eventually he would like it to go to his children. He makes a will to this effect. He dies first and Sally inherits the country home, but instead of making a will and leaving the home to the children, Sally sells the home.

In both of the above cases, a properly drawn up will could have ensured a distribution of the estate which was closer to the individual's wishes. It is possible for a will to cater for the situation of a beneficiary dying shortly after the deceased so that the property passes according to the original will rather than that of the beneficiary. A will can also allow for a beneficiary dying before the testator. Unless a will allows for this, the property meant for the deceased beneficiary would form part of what is known as the residuary estate (the rest of the testator's property which hasn't been specifically designated for particular beneficiaries) or in some cases the property may have to be passed according to the laws of intestacy. Instead a will could specify the property goes to a named beneficiary, but if that beneficiary predeceases the testator, it is to be passed to another named beneficiary.

Mutual wills aim to prevent the situation described in Simon and Sally's case. Simon wanted the property to go to his wife, but eventually to his children, but after inheriting, Sally sold the house. If they had made mutual wills and discussed what they both needed and wanted, it would have been possible for both of them to prepare similar wills so that, whichever one of them died first, eventually the house would have passed to the children.

Besides being professionally drawn up by a solicitor, a will should be regularly reviewed to take into account any changes in circumstances such as the birth of a child or the death of an intended beneficiary, or separation from a partner.

If a couple marry after making a will, the marriage makes the will invalid so a new one will need to be made even if all the circumstances are the same. The only exception to this is if the will was made in contemplation of the marriage. The will needs to state that this is the case, and the marriage must be a definite event rather than a vague possibility.

Summary

Some couples live together as a sort of 'trial marriage'; others may live together as an alternative to marriage permanently, or as a temporary measure because there is some legal impediment to their getting married – usually that one or both of them are still legally married to another person.

As explained throughout this book, couples who plan to live together for only a short period of time need to make arrangements as much as couples who plan to live together permanently as an alternative to marriage because living together is never a simple 'no ties' alternative to marriage. Property and money will mingle and probably muddle as well, rights and responsibilities may change or increase; all these things need to be thought about and plans made to protect oneself as an individual and also each other.

However, what will happen to these arrangements when the couple do marry? The law of marriage is just as complex as the law affecting couples who live together, but the following is an indication of the main areas that will be affected by getting married.

Cohabitation contracts

These become invalid on marriage as the law makes provisions instead and does not recognise pre-nuptial contracts or agreements of this nature.

Wills and intestacy

A will is invalidated by a subsequent marriage unless it states that it was made in contemplation of marriage to a specific person. The partner becomes next of kin on marriage.

Children

A mother's rights and responsibilities are unaffected. A father will gain equal rights and responsibilities towards his children automatically on marriage.

Property

If a couple own a home jointly, they will continue to own it either as joint tenants or tenants in common the same as before they were married. If a couple hold the property as tenants in common and one spouse dies intestate, the surviving spouse will inherit the deceased spouse's share as he or she will now be next of kin.

If only one spouse owns the property, the other spouse will have a right to live in the property for the duration of the marriage and can register this right. A court has greater discretion to determine property ownership and division of the proceeds of sale on the break up of a marriage compared to the separation of a couple who were living together.

If a couple rent property, both now have the right to live there and have rent accepted by the landlord even if only one of them is named on the lease.

Maintenance

Spouses are responsible for the maintenance of each other.

Tax

Spouses are taxed independently of each other, but the husband is entitled to the Married Couple's Allowance. If full use is not made of the allowance the wife can use the allowance against her income.

Widow's pension

The widow's pension is a pension paid to a widow who is under the age of 45, without dependants, who was married and whose husband has died. She will continue to receive this pension for as long as she remains alone. If she remarries or cohabits, she will lose this pension. If her marriage ends, payment of the pension will not resume, but if her cohabitation ends then the pension will resume. This might affect her decision whether to remarry or cohabit.

How to Find Out More Information

Child Support Agency
This is part of the Department of Social Security and can be contacted through your local DSS office. It is also listed under 'Child Support Agency' in the telephone directory.

Citizens' Advice Bureaux
See under 'Citizens' Advice Bureaux' in the telephone directory.

Council housing
You should apply to the Housing Department of your local council for this.

Council tax benefit
You should apply to the council tax benefit office of your local council.

Courts
See under 'Courts' in the telephone directory for all types of courts.

Department of Social Security
See under 'Benefits Agency' in the telephone directory.

District Land Registry
For the address of your nearest land registry see under 'Land

Registry' in the telephone directory. The nearest land registry may not be the one that deals with your property but they will be able to direct you to the correct one.

Homelessness
If you are about to become homeless you should apply to the homeless persons unit of your local council.

Housing benefit
You should apply to the housing benefit office of your local council.

Land Charges Registry
Contact the Superintendent, Land Charges Department, Burrington Way, Plymouth, PL5 3LP to register your right as a non-owning spouse.

Letting agencies and accommodation agencies
The best place to find these is in local newspapers. The *Yellow Pages* will also list them.

Registering births
See under 'Registration of Births, Marriages and Deaths' in the telephone directory.

Relate
Formerly known as the Marriage Guidance Council. See under 'Relate' in the telephone directory, or phone their head office on 01788 573241.

Rent Assessment Committee
See under 'Rent' in the telephone directory.

Securities and Investments Board
To check whether a financial adviser is authorised to give financial advice, ask at the central register of the Securities and Investments Board, Gavrelle House, 2–14 Bunhill Row, London, EC1Y 8RA (0171-638 1240).

Solicitors

The *Yellow Pages*, the Law Society and most Citizens' Advice Bureaux will have lists of local solicitors. Alternatively, most firms in the high street will be able to handle the matters dealt with in this book. Not all do legal aid.

Further reading from Kogan Page

Good Retirement Guide, Rosemary Brown, annual.

How to Cope with Separation and Divorce, David Green, 1995.

How to Write a Will and Gain Probate, Marlene Garsia, Fifth edition, 1995.

Splitting Up: A Legal and Financial Guide to Separation and Divorce, David Green, Third edition, 1995.

Index